500 TIPS

for Research Students

SALLY BROWN, LIZ McDOWELL
AND PHIL RACE

KOGAN
PAGE

London • Philadelphia

Kogan Page Limited
120 Pentonville Road
London N1 9JN

© Sally Brown, Liz McDowell and Phil Race

British Library Cataloguing in Publication Data

A CIP record for this book is available from the British Library.

ISBN 0 7494 1767 6

Typeset by Saxon Graphics, Derby
Printed and bound in Great Britain by Biddles Ltd, Guildford and King's Lynn

Contents

Preface and Acknowledgements

Starting to do research can happen at a stage in your life when you're flushed with success, for example after getting a good first degree. Alternatively, it may be the beginning of the realisation of a long-held ambition, or it may seem like the next logical step in your academic career.

Research is essentially about doing things that haven't been done before, so it's not possible to write a book which can tell you exactly how to become good at it all. What we've therefore tried to do here is to use our experience as researchers (and as supervisors of research, and examiners of higher degree students) to put together over 500 'tips'. These are meant to be pointers in the right direction towards taking on the challenges of being a research student, rather than a recipe for successful researching. The very nature of research varies enormously from one discipline to another, and the best advice regarding research methodologies should come from your supervisor and other people working in your field. While in this book we make no claim to be able to help you with the intricacies in your own research field, we do hope that we can help you make better use of these people. More importantly, we hope this book will help you to tune in to being involved in research, and to put into clear perspective the milestones along the way of assembling your findings and heading towards a research degree.

It was very hard for us to decide what the best order would be to present over fifty sets of tips, not least because there are times when you may need help in settling in, help in getting your research under way, help in approaching the teaching side of your work, and help in starting to put together the products of your research – often all at the same time!

This book is not therefore intended to be read from cover to cover at any one time. We think you will find it best to use the contents page and index to track down the sections that are of most immediate relevance to you on a day to day basis. We hope you will find our book a valuable companion throughout your period of doing research, and something to dip into all along the way. We also hope that our book will provide comfort and motivation during the darker days which may befall, from time to time, anyone engaged in extended research, even if this only comes from the satisfaction of recognising how many things you are doing right already.

We thank many friends and colleagues for their enthusiasm for the idea of a book of tips for researchers. We are particularly grateful to Hazel Fullerton who gave valuable feedback on the sections relating to teaching. We are also very grateful to Peter Knight for detailed and valuable comments on many of the research aspects of this book. We are indebted to Alan Jenkins for posing us some challenging questions about the nature of research and the sort of help that research students particularly need. We are encouraged by many comments along the lines 'if only there'd been something like this when I was a research student', and for valuable suggestions from several colleagues and research students, in particular Maxine Alterio, Julie Mortimer, Janet Wellard and Martin Davies.

Sally Brown, Liz McDowell and Phil Race
University of Northumbria at Newcastle
August 1995

Chapter 1 Getting Started In Research

The first two chapters of this book are about starting off your life as a research student. We've collected together in Chapter 1 our suggestions about getting your research going, and saved for Chapter 2 ideas about tuning in to your new surroundings and managing your time and effort.

We start this chapter by inviting you to interrogate yourself about your reasons for getting into research in the first place. The better your reasons for doing research, the more likely you are to succeed. We then give suggestions concerning the key decisions about the nature and direction of your research, which you'll need to make sooner or later. Next we look at dealing with supervisors – very important people in the overall picture for any researcher.

The remainder of this chapter deals with different aspects that you'll need to consider as your work develops, including planning, piloting and trialling, and coping with difficulties. We've also included some suggestions particularly for part-time students. These may apply to anyone who has got a lot of commitments to balance alongside their research work.

We've also looked at how to make the most of fellow research students. You will probably become integrated within a new community of colleagues and friends, and the more you put in to making this community work well, the better will be your experience of being a research student.

Research students usually have tales to tell of things that go wrong. We think that, rather than pretend that such things will never happen to you, it is better to confront them right from the outset, and this will help you to put them into a more healthy perspective.

1

Why are you doing research?

You may be embarking on research full-time shortly after completing a degree course or after a career break, or you may be planning to undertake research alongside a full-time or part-time job. Whatever your particular circumstances, you need to identify and maintain you motivations for doing research to sustain you through what is bound to be a lengthy project. Why might **you** want to do research? We've listed ten possible reasons why you might choose to do research; all the better if you've got strong reasons of your own.

1. **A career move.** A research degree may be the stepping stone to the career you want in some fields. Many scientific careers and most academic careers require you to have a research degree.

2. **Personal interest.** The research may give you the chance to explore an issue which is a great personal interest to you.

3. **Following someone's example.** You may have friends or relatives who have done research, and want to emulate their example.

4. **Because other people expect you to do research.** This may not be the best reason for starting on research – you really need reasons of your own for doing it to help you keep going when the going gets tough.

5. **Avoiding the 'real world'.** Doing research does give you more independence, freedom and flexibility than most jobs – but it doesn't pay very well! It may give you the chance to stay in or get back into academic life – though if you are expecting a continuation of undergraduate student living you may find yourself in for a surprise.

6. **Because you can't find a job, or know it's going to be hard to get one.** A research degree (or some research experience) may increase your chances of being appointed to jobs you would like to secure. A period doing research may give you time to decide exactly what you want to do next.

7   **Developing your skills and abilities.** Doing research provides lots of opportunities to develop skills and abilities which are transferable to other career and life situations. Some of these might include: problem-solving, using initiative, working independently, sifting through information, and making decisions.

8   **You enjoy doing research.** You may already have some research experience and know that this is one of the most interesting and exciting ways of spending your time. In fact, you're already hooked!

9   **Pure vanity!** Many people study for doctorates because they want to be called 'Doctor'! This is not a bad reason, in fact, as it usually represents a strong personal desire to succeed. Alternatively, your motive may be proving to yourself that you can do it. You may feel that a research degree is the next step on the educational ladder – and you want to get right to the top of it!

10   **Because you like working with the unknown.** This is a healthy basis for choosing to do research, and it lessens any tendencies to be frustrated by uncertainties.

2

Making key research decisions

When you begin a research project there are a lot of decisions to be made. You need to decide on the exact topic for your research and how to approach it, then come the details of experimental or survey design. Since many of these decisions loom large at the beginning of a project when you may feel you know very little, it can be daunting.

1 **Nothing is final.** Decisions you are asked to make at the beginning may seem to be irrevocable but often research changes in minor ways, and sometimes in major ways, as it goes along. This is an accepted part of the research process.

2 **Have an escape route.** Consider alternatives if the idea you first thought of doesn't work. Try to think through the consequences of your decisions. It is always worth having Plan B. Or you could try doing more than one thing in parallel for a while and see how they work out.

3 **Don't rush your decisions.** You may begin to panic if the days and weeks are slipping by and you don't feel you are actually doing anything. Don't let this feeling push you into action for the sake of action. Thinking and planning does take time. Play with ideas for a day or two and see how they feel.

4 **Don't start from scratch.** Somebody else has almost certainly undertaken a similar project, needed a similar piece of measuring equipment or done a similar kind of survey. Do your best to find out. Research is all about building on the work of others.

5 **Write it down.** Writing down and trying to express clearly what you want to do and how you intend to achieve it is probably the most useful way of clarifying and pinning down your thoughts.

6   **Get a second opinion.** And a third and fourth! Write down your ideas, plans, rationale and first thoughts and get others to look at them. They may well notice some things that you have overlooked. Your research supervisors should be particularly helpful here.

7   **Doing research is about progressively focused decision-making.** Don't expect to get everything sorted out once and for all and then simply get on with it. You will find yourself constantly facing decisions about what to do next, how to interpret this set of data, what is significant and so on.

8   **Don't wait till you know what you're going to do is the best possible course of action.** Do something anyway. Sometimes deciding to do something is better than waiting to be sure that you are doing the right thing (but see 'escape route' above).

9   **Keep a sense of proportion.** Research isn't your whole life and in the overall scheme of things, will it destroy the planet if you make a wrong choice? Time spent doing research is an opportunity to get an overview of the field you're interested in before making important choices.

10 **Take responsibility.** It's your project. No one else can or should make the important decisions for you. However, listen to people who have fallen into the pits that can trap the unwary, as they know where the pits are, and how to avoid them.

3

Choosing your supervisor

Some researchers are able to choose who to ask to supervise their research. Other research projects are devised by a senior academic who sometimes also obtains funding to employ a researcher. In this situation you don't have much choice about your first supervisor but you may be able to choose a second supervisor.

1   **The eminent professor may also be an absent professor.** The most eminent person in the field is not necessarily the best supervisor, though others may be impressed to hear that you are working with him or her.

2   **Keep first impressions in perspective.** It's all too easy to be attracted towards choosing someone who comes across immediately as approachable and friendly, or to steer away from someone who seems rather aloof or formal. What matters ultimately is how good these people turn out to be as supervisors.

3   **Find out about supervision success rates – and failures.** A supervisor who has already had successful researchers is less of a risk (though of course every supervisor has to have a first research student).

4   **Talk to other researchers.** If you are considering approaching someone to ask them to be your research supervisor it helps if you can talk first to someone else who has been supervised by them. Find out from them how frequently they see their supervisor.

5   **Prepare your shopping list!** It's useful when talking to other researchers about how they get on with their supervisors, to have your own set of questions to help you decide who will be most likely to get on with you.

6   **Ask other lecturers.** They may have some good ideas of who would be a good person to supervise on the topic you're going to research. You will probably also be able to read between the lines what lecturers think about each other. This can help you avoid being the lonely research student supervised by the lecturer that no colleagues like very much.

7   **Take the initiative.** In many situations you don't have to wait for a supervisor to be allocated. You can ask the person you think would suit you best. They won't mind, will probably be flattered and can only say 'No'.

8   **Think about possibilities of complementary supervisors.** In many universities you are required to have more than one supervisor. It's useful if they can complement each other. One may be eminent and give status but have very little time for you. Another may have more time and be closer to the experience of being a new researcher.

9   **Read the regulations.** Your university may have regulations about who can act as a research supervisor. For example, lecturers registered for part-time PhDs probably aren't eligible, no matter how relevant and extensive their experience. In most universities, supervision arrangements have to be registered and approved by an appropriate committee or board.

10   **Find out the groundrules.** Check out with potential supervisors their expectations of their research students. Gently probe whether they are likely to meet your own expectations and needs. See if there are any university codes of practice for research supervision.

4

Dealing with your supervisor

Your supervisor is probably one of the most important people in a crucial phase of your life. You may even have more than one person sharing the supervision of your work. Supervisors are allegedly human beings, and the following suggestions may help you get on with them.

1   **Develop some groundrules.** Establish at the beginning what you can expect from your supervisor and what he or she expects in return. This might include how often you will meet, how you should arrange other urgent meetings, what kind of reports of progress you are to submit, how quickly your supervisor will respond to written material you submit for comment and so on.

2   **Know your university's policy and guidelines.** There is almost certain to be a policy on research supervision and perhaps a set of minimum standards. If you are aware of them you will know whether you are getting a fair deal, and what is reasonably expected of you yourself.

3   **Supervisors tend to disagree!** When you have more than one research supervisor it is not uncommon for them to disagree. Depending on how important the matter is, you can consider their different views and decide for yourself, or you get them together to discuss the points of disagreement and negotiate a joint way forward. Don't make enemies by playing up their disagreements with each other. Or try a third party.

4   **Keep records of meetings.** Your supervisor may or may not be very good at keeping a record of what you discussed and agreed. To make sure there is no confusion, keep a written record of points agreed and actions to be taken. Send your supervisor a copy.

5   **Changing your supervisor is usually an option.** It is not unknown for researchers to change their supervisors and most universities have a policy on this. If serious problems arise make use of this – but don't start initiating such changes the first time you fall out with your supervisor – and don't automatically blame your supervisor when you're stressed or drowning!

6   **Remember that it is your research.** Your supervisor will not expect you to go along to meetings to be told what to do. The meetings are for you to test out ideas and to obtain guidance when you need it. It is up to you to let your supervisor know what you need and to take charge of your own project. Don't skip meetings! There is a temptation to avoid meetings when things are not going very well. You may intend to see your supervisor next week when everything is sorted out – but it usually gets worse! If you force your supervisor into having to track you down it can be a real mess!

7   **Take care with the boundaries.** Many supervisors spend at least some time socialising informally with their research students. Avoid the temptation to translate free-and-easy attitudes from social times to work times.

8   **Become better at receiving critical feedback.** If you're defensive or hostile, you may stem the flow of feedback from your supervisor. All feedback is useful, even when we feel we disagree with it. Accept praise too! People who give compliments don't like them being 'shrugged off' by the recipient. Build on positive feedback, and allow it to give you a positive feeling about your work.

10 **Don't be too proud to say 'sorry'!** Any relationship between human beings has its difficult times, and the effect of these is minimised when they are confronted rather than buried. You may know more about your subject than your supervisor, but *not* more about getting a higher degree successfully.

5

Planning your research

Whatever you plan to do in your research, things will change as the research develops. This is no excuse for not planning. As somebody once said 'Plans are useless but planning is absolutely vital' – and as someone else once said 'to fail to plan is to plan to fail!'.

1   **Take advice.** Your research supervisors know about the stages you need to plan for in your research and roughly how long things will take. They will also know the main phases you should allow for in your plans.

2   **Don't underestimate the time it will take to settle in.** Make your early plans reasonable, and don't put yourself under pressure to achieve too much in the early stages.

3   **Take charge of your time, don't let time rule you.** Make your plans flexible and firm at the same time. Give yourself definite dates by which you (reasonably) intend to complete each phase of your research. Keep your plans visible – set your deadlines out on a wall chart or in a diary.

4   **Remember that in life in general many things get done in the last 10% of the available time.** This means, in fact, that they can be done in much less time than might have been anticipated. This in turn means that you can get a surprising amount done in *any* 10% of your total time allocation – plan not to depend on that last 10%. Plan a few concentrated work binges – then fun!

5   **Allow for piloting and trialling.** It is very important not to rush into the main stages of your research because you think you are short of time. Piloting is expected and important. Allow for muddles, computer bugs, false starts, and red herrings.

6   **Allow time for writing up.** This is so often forgotten in the excitement of collecting and analysing data. And remember that by the time you get to the writing up stage you may well also be looking for a job.

7   **Display your plan.** Show your plan in a chart on the wall or on your computer so that you can see where you should be – and (if you're brave) so that other people can see where you intend to be at each stage.

8   **Discuss your plans on an ongoing basis.** Sharing your plans with your supervisor and with fellow researchers can help you ensure that your plans are achievable.

9   **Make good use of 'early' time.** When you find yourself ahead of schedule, don't just sit back. Bring forward other elements from your total plan, and build on your successes.

10 **Don't panic when you're running late.** Research is the sort of activity where you should expect some things to take much longer than you expected. Other aspects will take less time than you expect. Sometimes, everyone has setbacks, such as a couple of weeks off due to 'flu. Allow yourself to be human, and to have ups and downs.

6

Piloting and trialling

Before spending a lengthy period of time and perhaps going to some expense to collect data, it is usual to undertake a pilot or trial. This enables you try out your method of data collection whether it be a survey, interviews, or using a piece of measuring equipment in a laboratory. Before you go any further you can find out whether the method works, whether it provides you with the data you want and what you can do with that data.

1 **Recruit your friends.** Also don't hesitate to bring in your neighbours and the people at the bus stop, if you need people on whom to try out your questionnaires or interviews. But remember that people in a pilot should be as similar as possible to the people you will be contacting in the main project. You might start with friends as a pre-pilot and then move on to a more appropriate group.

2 **Allow sufficient time.** It always takes longer than you think to set up a process for collecting data and carrying it out. Remember that after you have trialled a method or collected pilot data you need time to reflect on it and analyse it if you are to learn from it in order to design your main study.

3 **Clarify exactly what you're trying to measure.** Don't be afraid to face up to the possibility that you're not yet trying to measure the right things! Ask other people whether they think there are other things you should be trying to test out along with your early attempts. Don't expect to get everything right first time. You are almost inevitably going to be doing something new. New things don't usually work right first time. This is why you need piloting or trialling.

4 **Remember that with questionnaires, you may only get the answers to the questions you ask.** Other things may be more important, so include open ended, free response questions from which to gather other factors that may be worth following up in future questionnaires or interviews.

5   **Beware of setting yourself up.** It's all too easy when you think you know what you're going to measure, quite subconsciously to skew your methodology in a way that confirms your own expectations.

6   **Save some for later.** Don't involve all the people you want to contact in your main project in the pilot study. Save the most relevant people for when you've given your methodology a test-run, and improved your approaches.

7   **Keep your pilot data.** You may be able to use your pilot data as part of your main project, so take some care with it. Keep it safe and well-documented. It's often worth reporting your pilot study along with the changes you made in later work based on your first findings. It's worth writing up your pilot data (for stress release and later reflection) including feelings and thoughts that aren't yet totally formed.

8   **Don't overdo the statistical analysis.** If you've only got a fairly small collection of data, there's little value to be derived from working out standard deviations and levels of significance from it. It's probably better to concentrate on qualitative findings and descriptive statistics from small sets of data, and save complex statistical analysis for your main study, if it is appropriate.

9   **Expect the need to re-interpret your data.** As you find out more about what you're studying, you are likely to see deeper significances even in data which at first sight seemed quite straightforward. That is the nature of research.

10   **Write up your methods** *now*. You're otherwise likely to forget *why* you did things in the ways you chose, and why they made the best possible sense.

7

Using other people as a resource

Other people are your most valuable resource in completing your research successfully. And usually they want to help, so don't be afraid to admit that you're just learning how to do research and seek their views. We'll look later at working with fellow research students in particular, but first let's look at how you can use other people in general.

1 **Get an expert to talk to you.** If you can find people who have some specialism or expertise relevant to your research, talk to them about it. Experts usually love to talk about their pet subjects and will give their time freely. Better still, collar intelligent non-experts, and try to explain to them what you are doing.

2 **Use conferences to identify more people to try to talk to.** Conferences are particularly valuable as you can usually manage to talk to 'famous' people quite informally in coffee-breaks and in the bar – as well as attending their sessions.

3 **Make full use of your fellow-researchers.** Forget any feelings of competing with them regarding who's to get finished first! You *all* want to finish successfully, and you share the same goals, problems, and triumphs. The commentary of critical friends is really useful.

4 **Don't forget the support staff in your department.** Technicians, administrative and secretarial staff may have the skills and knowledge to help you in certain areas and they like to be consulted too. For example ask the secretaries for help on how to get the most from your word processor, and how to go about organising your filing. Technical staff may be able to point you towards valuable short cuts regarding experimental techniques.

5   **Go to a lecture.** If you are attached to a university or college there will be lots of courses going on, some of which may provide you with just the background knowledge, or the skills in a new area which you need. As a researcher you may well be able to join in some classes for free.

6   **Don't adopt the ostrich position.** Talk to everyone you can about your research, especially any problems you are having so that you can get feedback on them. Do a good turn whenever you can. If you can be helpful and useful to other people, they may be more likely to help you out when you need it. Besides, it does a lot for one's self-esteem to feel that one is helping other people.

7   **Network!** Join networks of researchers, start some correspondence with people who write about your subject, use the Internet. You don't have to be reliant on people on the spot. There's a whole community of people out there who share your interests.

8   **Identify the end-users.** If your research is relevant to a particular profession, industry or community group make contacts there and get them to give their opinions on your research and help its progress along. Also identify and talk to the 'secondary users' – others who may be tangentially affected by the outcomes of your research work.

9   **Don't be too proud to be trained.** Your university may have research methods courses that are well worth attending – if not in your own department, check whether such courses exist elsewhere. If necessary, look further afield, for example at Economic and Social Research Council (ESRC) training courses elsewhere.

10 **Remember, it's 'other people' who will eventually judge your work.** The more you have talked about your work all the way through with other people, the less the risk of unpleasant surprises at the end of the day.

8

Some tips for part-time researchers

Most of the ideas in this book are relevant to students researching for higher degrees part-time. However, if you're in this position, you'll already know that there are additional factors to be considered. We hope the following suggestions will be particularly useful to you – if not all welcome at first sight.

1   **It seems like it will take forever!** Do you really want to do it? It takes a great deal more courage and perseverance to work towards a higher degree part-time. It's only too easy to become dispirited and fall by the wayside the first time there's a real problem.

2   **Are your 'significant others' right with you?** This is absolutely vital. If there's a possibility that the demands on your time and energies of researching part-time may jeopardise your arrangements with your partner or family, you will may have to make crucial decisions about what's most important to all concerned. Be careful to work out what's in it for them in the long term, and not just for you – and discuss such things openly.

3   **Is your employer behind you?** There could well be times when your research and your job could cause conflicting pressures. You will almost certainly need to keep your job to finance your studies.

4   **Will your access to resources be sufficient?** Check that you'll find it possible to get at library and computer resources adequately. Your boss at work may be able to help to provide you with space to study at work in quiet time, and access to equipment.

5   **Do a 'time audit' for a 'normal' week.** Map out how you spend each hour or half-hour. Headings such as 'social', 'job', 'family', 'home upkeep', 'hobbies', 'sleep' and 'eating' may be useful. Then work out how much time you *could* realistically divert to research in a typical week – still leaving some spare time for the unexpected!

6 **Do a skills audit.** You may already have developed several skills crucial to effective research in the course of your job or career. Think of things such as using libraries, report-writing, giving presentations, working with other people, problem-solving and so on.

7 **Remember your strengths.** These could include that you're already good at managing your time, being self-motivated, working in isolation at times, doing several things concurrently, and taking responsibility for your own work.

8 **Talk to other part-time researchers already under way.** Ask them what the *real* problems turned out to be that they hadn't considered. Also ask them about the problems they expected, but which turned out to be insignificant.

9 **Make sure your supervisor knows what it's like to research part-time.** Think twice about working with a supervisor whose only experience is with full-time research students.

10 **Find out what it will all cost.** Check carefully about different sorts of fees, and whether you'll have to pay towards costs of resources. You may also have to take into account potential reductions in your earnings, if your availability for work (for example overtime) is significantly affected.

9

Working with fellow research students

There are advantages and disadvantages regarding working alongside other research students. We hope the following suggestions will help you make the most of them – and avoid some of the potential pitfalls.

1 **Remember that it's quite a close relationship.** If you're sharing a room or laboratory with other research students, you'll need to rub along successfully for a number of years perhaps. Fellow-researchers can be a valuable support network. These are people who understand what you're doing, and share your aims and ambitions. Take special care not to get off to a bad start with them.

2 **Share ideas and information.** It can be useful to discuss your research with other researchers working on similar topics as it goes along. If you are working on closely related projects you may even be able to help each other with literature searching, passing on useful references, and writing joint papers.

3 **Beware of competitiveness.** It will often seem as though everyone's cleverer, harder-working, and making more progress than you! Really there's no need for competition. You're all intending to succeed, not just some of you. You're all allowed to succeed, not just the best of you! It's sometimes hard to adjust to this absence of competition after your experiences as an undergraduate when you may have felt you were competing regarding classification of your degree.

4 **One year is a long time in research.** If you find yourself as a new researcher, sharing space or facilities with someone who has been there a year longer, don't underestimate how much such people will have learned in that year. They can be less than patient with a cocky new spacemate who seems to know it all!

5   **Help with practical tasks.** Fellow researchers may be able to keep an eye on your experiment if you have to go out for a while. They can pass on messages, proof read an article, or check some of your calculations – as long as you are willing to do the same for them when the need arises.

6   **Don't be too dependent on already established researchers** (such as people coming to the end of their research degree programmes, or employed as Post-docs). Though they may be able to give you all sorts of help and support, remember they have their own research to do! They can get tetchy if continually asked for advice.

7   **Accept help when it is offered.** If someone sees you struggling and wants to assist, refusing such help can seem a real snub, and may prevent you from being offered further help in the future when you may really need it.

8   **Keep socialising in its place.** You may get on so well with your fellow researchers that you all spend a lot of time chatting, drinking coffee, going out at lunchtime.You do need time off, but make sure it's also possible to get on with some research work in peace and quiet without being made to feel anti-social.

9   **Respect other people's preferences.** This may involve things such as smoking, whether windows or blinds stay open or closed, whether the heating is turned up or down, and other such things. If things aren't to your satisfaction, tackle one issue at a time, and carefully.

10 **Don't tell tales to teacher!** Researchers who grumble to their supervisors about fellow-researchers usually lose quite a lot of respect from their supervisors, and may make permanent enemies of the person who is grumbled about. Researchers who grumble about their supervisors either have a death wish, or should change supervisors pretty damn quick!

10

What to do when things go wrong

What if all your questionnaires are sent out with the wrong return address labels? What if your data logging equipment is stolen and you lose all your data? What if the organisation in which you are working refuses to allow continued access?

1   **Don't panic!** Most situations are retrievable and this kind of thing has happened to other researchers before you. However, most people don't talk about them and they certainly don't get written into final reports! Some of your network contacts might have had similar experiences and be able to help.

2   **Take a break.** Try to regain your perspective. There are other things in your life than this research – if not, rectify the balance *now!*

3   **Have a fall back position.** Try to plan for some alternative approaches so that if something does go wrong you have a chance to retrieve things. When planning and doing fieldwork, build in some deliberate redundancy, so that you're not dependent on every single part of your work.

4   **Take stock.** Even if you have lost some data, or been prevented from collecting some of the information you had hoped for, it may be that in fact you can still achieve a satisfactory outcome. As a perfectionist, you probably thought you needed all that data but maybe the research can actually stand up without it. Data does get lost, especially if information technology (IT) based, even if you have three generations of computer files in different locations. It will happen to you too!

5   **Two steps forward, one step backwards.** This tends to be the nature of research. Don't assume that a particular step backwards equates to final disaster – it may just be part of the natural 'growing pains' accompanying successful research.

6 **Don't pretend that you haven't got any problems.** Talk to your supervisor, and to other research students you know. People are usually most understanding when they can see genuine difficulties or problems, and will offer useful advice.

7 **Get an extension.** You will probably have a deadline for the completion of your research. However, most academic departments will give extensions to this deadline for real disasters and genuine problems. Contact your supervisors as soon as possible.

8 **Do it better this time.** If you have to re-do something, take the opportunity to improve on the way you did it the first time. You may end up with a better, and more concise, piece of research following your disaster.

9 **Capture what you learned from adversity.** The fact that things did not work out initially may provide you with rich discussion material for your thesis, about adjustments to initial approaches, learning from experience, and strategic planning of research. Worry about people whose theses tell the story of model pieces of problem-free research!

10 **Remember that what didn't work is often just as interesting as what did.** There is room in any thesis for a critical account of unsuccessful approaches to solving a problem, alongside the tactics that finally paid off.

11

Avoiding disasters

There are some common problems that researchers encounter. Don't imagine that it can't happen to you. Take note. The disasters we've mentioned below all refer to research processes one way or another, but don't forget that there are other kinds of disaster which can be even more serious, such as illness, divorce, all sorts of things to do with children, broken computers, financial disasters... but dealing with all of these would take another book, so we'll have to stick to research disasters!

1   **Lack of proper piloting and trialling.** The purpose of piloting is to avoid disasters in collecting and analysing the data for your research; make sure you do enough.

2   **Inadequate planning.** Even though it is difficult to plan everything about your research at the beginning, you need to plan as carefully as you can, and continually monitor and modify your plans.

3   **Failing to do a comprehensive literature search.** A common disaster is to find a vital piece of previous research with really significant implications for your project when it is too late to take it into account. This can cause serious problems, so do your literature searching thoroughly.

4   **Failing to keep track of the emerging literature.** Another cause of disaster is when someone else is working on the same problem or issue as you are – and publishes first! The sooner you're alerted to this, the sooner you can change your own plans and approaches to ensure that you do something original and new.

5   **Beware of 'I've started, so I'll finish!'** When circumstances change, it's usually best to make new research plans, or substantially adapt your existing ones, than to stick rigidly to your first intentions. For example, if important new work in your area is published, replan your own work to take it into account or build on it, rather than pretend it never happened!

6   **Failing to negotiate access.** Many research projects have faced disaster when someone 'in authority' puts a block on the work. If you are undertaking research in any kind of organisation such as a school, a business, or voluntary organisation, make sure that you have a written agreement, ratified by a senior person, about what you will be allowed to do, what facilities will be offered to you and so on.

7   **Running out of time.** It is very common for there to be no time at the end of a project for writing it up. Perhaps the most important thing is to know when to stop collecting data so that you can allow yourself the time you need to write up. Don't forget that you're ultimately judged on the basis of what you write up – not on everything you did or thought of doing.

8   **Beware of thinking 'I'll get a job, and do the writing up as soon as I can'.** Moving to a new job and a new place takes more time and energy than you may think, and the deadline for submitting your work may approach surprisingly quickly.

9   **What if I fail?** It would seem like a disaster if you submitted your thesis and it did not pass but in fact there are almost always opportunities to do some rewriting and re-submit. This is one disaster you can avoid by getting drafts to your supervisors in good time and paying attention to their comments.

10   **Remind yourself that 'failure' is quite rare.** Non-completion is more common! If you really want to succeed in gaining a higher degree, you are likely to achieve your ambition. Don't let *anything* stop you!

Chapter 2 Finding Your Feet – And Keeping Them

This chapter is about survival and progress. We start by looking at how you may best try to settle in to a new institution, and also into the department, section or school where your research work will be based. Starting doing research is a major transition for most people – a bit like the transition you've already experienced when first going to university from school. In both cases, it may have seemed as if you were comfortably settled in to a group of people all doing the same thing, when suddenly you found that you were the 'new person' in a world of people all seeming to know a lot more than you do!

In this chapter we look at a variety of the hazards of being a researcher, including uncertainty, boredom, inertia and isolation. Starting researching does not mean that you've finished studying, so we give some tips about developing your study skills accordingly, although these may well be rather different from the study skills you developed as an undergraduate. We also look at time – something that you'll often feel is in short supply.

We've included in this chapter some suggestions about recording and logging your research activities. In a way, we could have placed these suggestions in any of the first three chapters of this book, but we chose to put them here because an effective way of keeping track of your work is as much a coping strategy as a research process.

We end this chapter with some general tips about how to look after yourself in a global sense throughout the period of your research. Suggestions here may avoid you getting run down and depressed – something that seems to happen quite frequently to research students, often quite avoidably.

12

Develop your institutional know-how

Several of the sets of tips in this book suggest you getting into the main activities of your department. In this set, we suggest some more general ideas relating to the overall operation of your university.

1   **Find out about the academic values of your university.** Different universities have different traditions and practices. It's useful to tune into the ethos of your university. This helps you to become accepted, rather than stand out like a sore thumb. Read the mission statement if there's one in the prospectus. Talk to people.

2   **Find out how the committee structures work.** This may save you a lot of time trying to get something approved by the wrong committee! It's useful to know the timetables of any committees that you may need to use, and the ways to put proposals or suggestions to such committees.

3   **Explore the information technology facilities you may use.** Many universities have information technology centres containing resources and expertise which are unknown to many of the university staff, who could be putting them to good use.

4   **Find out all you need to know about accounts.** This may seem very boring, but it can save all sorts of hiccups when you need to put an order through a particular budget, or plan your requirements within existing constraints and timescales.

5   **Find out about deadlines that may affect you.** For example, your final 'research topic title' may have to be registered by a given date, and there may be timescales for submission of your thesis for final examination and viva.

6   **Explore your university's programme of study activities.** You may well wish to sign up for short courses or on-going programmes to develop skills and knowledge that could be useful in your future career. For example, there may be courses in wordprocessing, using computers, creative writing, report writing, and all sorts of other things if there's a Continuing Education or Extra Mural Department.

7   **See if there is training provision for research students.** Even if your own department does not provide such training, other departments may well do so for their own students, and would welcome you too. Courses in giving presentations, research methodology, and career planning may be particularly useful to you.

8   **Find out about the university's student support services.** Find where they're based, and go and browse to explore the leaflets they have to give away, which gives a good idea of the sorts of help they're geared up to provide for students. Such services are not confined to helping undergraduates – they often help staff with problems too.

9   **Find out who the university's most famous people are.** Such information may be gained by watching press releases, and scanning annual reports of research or publications. You may wish to go along to open lectures given by such people, and this could add significantly to your appreciation of the university.

10 **Find out what recreational facilities are available.** Many universities also have arrangements for discounts at local facilities. The Students' Union is usually a rich source of information about such things – and may be relaxingly peaceful out of term time.

13

Coping as the most inexperienced member of the department

It can come as a bit of a shock moving from being a student surrounded by people at a similar stage to yourself, to becoming part of the academic structure of a university. At worst, you may feel as if everyone has more knowledge and experience than you (though probably it's not that bad in fact!). The following suggestions may help you adjust to this change.

1   **Expect that lots of people will know a lot more than you yet know.** Don't try to pretend that you know more than you do.

2   **Be like a sponge for information and knowledge.** Absorb as much as you can from people around you. Don't rely on your memory; make notes of important or useful things you don't want to lose.

3   **Don't be afraid to ask people to explain things a bit more.** If you don't ask questions, people will assume that you understand things, and they can become impatient or frustrated if they later find out that you didn't understand all the way along.

4   **Don't be too much in awe of the distinguished people around you.** It can feel as though you'll never ever rise to the heights that they've achieved – but remember once each 'giant' was the least experienced person in some department.

5   **Take care, however, not to appear disrespectful.** Experienced staff can react adversely to new researchers who seem too cocky or confident. Try not to alienate anyone – you never know when their experience may be valuable to you.

6   **Try to get on with everyone.** There will often be people in the department who just can't stand each other, and it's only too easy for them to try to draw you into taking sides. Try to distance yourself from disagreements such people have with each other.

7   **Don't underestimate how rapidly your own experience will grow.** In the narrow confines of your particular research area, you'll soon have more experience than many of the people around you.

8   **When you find that you're lacking knowledge in something others know, take time out to look it up.** People around you will respect you for identifying knowledge gaps and rectifying them without being prompted to do so.

9   **Get on good terms with technical and support staff.** Be particularly careful that they don't feel that you take them for granted. Such staff will have really valuable experience and expertise, and you may well find them excellent allies in your work if they respect and like you.

10 **Look after the little courtesies.** Make sure that you take your turn to buy the coffee, get the sugar, and wash up the cups. Similarly, do at least your share of any other little chores, such as refilling the photocopier with paper, tidying up the place, and not spilling your papers into other people's space.

14

Coping with uncertainty

When you begin research you are venturing into something new so you may experience feelings of uncertainty. Will I have the ability to carry it out? Will I have anything worthwhile to say at the end? And you may wonder what you will do next after the research has finished. Research is usually only a short term phase in the life of most people – even though it may be a very crucial one.

1   **Take advice.** Other people can't run your research project for you but they can give you their advice and opinions. Make use of your supervisors and talk to other 'experts', fellow researchers, and anyone else who is willing to listen. Sometimes a non-expert opinion can be very useful (and usefully sobering!).

2   **Share your worries.** Talk to other researchers about how they are feeling. You will find that you are certainly not alone with your doubts and uncertainties. They tend to go with the researcher's territory.

3   **Do some easy things first.** Make sure you complete some tasks which you know you can cope with and which are definitely needed as part of the project. You might start with literature searching or designing a piece of equipment or learning how to use a software package.

4   **Have some short term goals.** Have some goals which are achievable in the short term so that you can check things off and see your own progress.

5   **Remember how to eat an elephant!** (The only way would be one bite at a time!) Working for a higher degree may seem like a mammoth task, but it's achieved in small, separate instalments.

6   **Remind yourself that it's very useful to have things you don't yet know.** When you have thought of some questions, you're already well on the way towards finding the answers to many of them. If you don't have any questions, you'll not find any answers.

7   **Find a fellow enthusiast.** Talk to someone who is really interested in the subject of your research. You are bound to be re-energised by talking to them and their interest will give your confidence a boost.

8   **Find a novice.** Talk to someone who knows nothing about your research (but is willing to give you a sympathetic ear). You'll be surprised at how much you have learnt and achieved already when you begin to explain to them what you are doing. Putting your ideas into words and getting them across is a valuable way for you to increase your understanding of your research.

9   **Enjoy the uncertainty.** If you're not uncertain, you're not learning! Doing research gives you a lot of freedom. You can decide how to organise your project and how to use your time. You have a great deal of scope intellectually. Enjoy it. If there wasn't at least some uncertainty, your research would be far too easy, and someone would already have done it!

10 **Allow yourself to grow by handling uncertainty.** Being able to tackle the unknown is a valuable life-skill as well as a useful research strategy. Probably the most important things you will get out of your research are not the results, but the personal growth that goes along with developing your approach to research.

15

Study skills tips for researchers

When you finished as an undergraduate, you may have thought your days of studying, in the normal sense of the word, were over! Not over, but different in fact. You've probably already got a good foundation regarding study skills, but the following suggestions may prove useful too.

1 **You'll still have to learn things!** However, much of what you now learn will not be formally taught to you. The responsibility for what you learn, how you learn, how fast you learn, and when you learn will mostly rest with you.

2 **There won't be a syllabus.** You'll have to work out the level to which you need to learn new things, and what will constitute evidence that you have succeeded.

3 **Your learning won't be driven by assessment.** (At least, not till towards the end of your researching!). When you start being responsible for pacing your own learning, you may realise for the first time what an important part exams, coursework-to-deadlines, reports-to-deadlines, and tests played in helping you pace your undergraduate studies.

4 **Make use of any 'formal' learning opportunities.** For example, if you're studying for a PhD straight from being an undergraduate, there may be related taught Masters programmes in your department. You will probably be welcomed to join such groups (without necessarily having to join in with any assessed work). You may even be required to participate fully. Such programmes can be quick ways of learning a lot about your new subjects.

5 **Plan in some time for studying.** Learning new things sometimes takes more effort than busily reading the literature or collecting data. Build into your typical week's activities some slots to devote to studying.

6   **Decide carefully what to study.** The most important thing is to identify things you really need to know – not just things which are nice to know because they're interesting.

7   **Ensure that your learning is active.** Don't just read things, hoping they will stay with you. Test out using ideas, solving problems, and practising new techniques straightaway.

8   **Be your own assessor.** Devise tests that let you prove to yourself that you have a firm grip on things you've been studying. Testing yourself on something you've learned is one of the best ways of identifying any gaps in your learning, as well as consolidating what you've learned successfully.

9   **Reflect on the efficiency of your studying.** You may not have found time to do this as an undergraduate. The more you know about what works for you when it comes to studying anything new, the more you can avoid wasting time and energy in your studies.

10 **Keep your hand in at demonstrating your learning.** If there are any exams or tests associated with any programmes you're studying alongside (for example, taught Masters programmes mentioned already) you may wish to have a go at the same tests or exams that the real candidates do (whether or not you actually put your work forward for assessment).

16

Organising your time

Usually research for a higher degree is spread over two, three or more years. With the end seeming so far away sometimes, it is very important to organise your time so that you continue to make progress.

1   **Remember Rome wasn't built in a day!** The business of research is on a much longer timescale than the terms or semesters that may have dominated your life for some years.

2   **Make a plan working back from the end of your project.** If you identify what has to be done in each stage of your project working back from final deadlines, you will realise how much has to be done now!

3   **Structure your day or week.** Having specific times when you will work on your research or on specific tasks helps to make sure that you don't continually put things off. Build into your plans times when you work more flexibly than other lecturers or students, so you can avoid queues in the library. Plan your access to specialised equipment or facilities so you can get easy access, when necessary making use of early or late parts of the day, or weekends.

4   **Have office hours for research time.** Research can easily take over your whole life or all of your free time. You may make better progress if you confine your research to specific times and at other times you are able to feel relaxed about getting away from it. However, expect to have to plan at least some of your research work outside 'normal' hours.

5   **Don't wait for inspiration.** If most of us waited for inspiration or until we were in the mood for planning, analysing or writing, we'd get very little done. Do it now! You can always revise and improve it later if needed.

6   **Set deadlines.** It helps if you have deadlines, even if you only create them for yourself. However you might pay more attention to deadlines you have agreed with other people such as your supervisors. Log your time. Then when you look back you can see how much you have achieved or resolve to do better, and plan how to approach improvements.

7   **Keep 'to do' lists.** In research there are often a lot of small tasks to do all going on at the same time. It's easy to forget things unless you keep a list. It is highly satisfying to cross off things that you've done from these lists!

8   **Allow time for thinking.** Doing things can too often be a poor substitute for thinking. Capture your thoughts. Think laterally. Use scratch pads, wacky-ideas lists, connections between very different things. Think theory.

9   **Don't get manic when things are working well!** Be pleased with yourself, of course, but don't feel you have to keep surging ahead with every ounce of your energy. Keep a grip, and make sure you don't sacrifice objectivity to enthusiasm.

10 **Build in safety margins.** Aim to complete each stage of your research a few weeks before you need to finish it. You never can tell when things outside your control can slow you down – family crises, illness, injury, or just plain bad luck.

17

Coping with boredom and inertia

Over the course of a lengthy project it would be surprising if you didn't feel bored or uninspired on some occasions. How can you re-energise yourself? Here are our suggestions.

1   **Talk to other researchers.** They know how you feel. They may be able to tell you all sorts of strategies they used to cope with the 'down' times in their research. Pick the strategies that suit you best.

2   **Keep in mind the outcomes of your research.** It can help to be in touch with people who you hope will eventually benefit from your research to remind you that it is worthwhile.

3   **Vary your day.** Don't do one thing for too long. Have some variety during the day. If you are doing some statistical analysis and become really fed up with the number-crunching, take time off to read some articles you've been meaning to look at.

4   **Take small bites.** Don't believe you have to do things in big chunks or spend whole days on one thing. Sometimes space in between helps.

5   **Expect days – or even weeks – when nothing goes right.** Sometimes it takes weeks to find out by trial and error how to perform an activity or experiment, and to repeat the successful piece of work will only take hours.

6   **Change your approach.** If something seems really boring then perhaps the approach is not the one for you. Is it really too late to change it and adapt? For example if you planned to base all your research on questionnaire data, perhaps you can also undertake some interviewing.

7 **Don't expect it all to be easy and straightforward.** If it were that easy, it would already have been done, and it would not be research. Boredom and inertia can be an escape mechanism, but you probably don't really want to escape!

8 **Remember that it's normal for research to be slower than learning about established knowledge.** Frontiers are usually slow to push back. Sometimes you'll make more progress in a day than you have done for weeks.

9 **Accept that you have the right to feel bored or inert!** Acknowledge that such feelings are perfectly normal human reactions to coping with the unknown or the unexpected. Avoid jumping to the conclusions that there must be something dreadfully wrong with you, or that you've got yourself into the wrong game.

10 **Do something useful anyway!** Times when your heart's not in it can be usefully spent tidying up your data and papers, sorting out your references, and paving the way for the next useful spurt forward. It can be useful to force yourself into commitments which will give you something definite to do – for example putting yourself forward to deliver a departmental seminar next month.

18

Coping with isolation

Being a researcher is not like being one of a group of undergraduate students and it is not like many regular jobs where you may work as a team with a group of colleagues. You can feel quite isolated. Here are some suggestions for overcoming this.

1   **Have a good social life.** Don't expect to find the same levels of companionship within the university or department which you may have enjoyed in your student days. As a researcher, you are part of a narrower community.

2   **Join a postgraduate society.** Find out if your university has such a society. You may find a number of people there who are in a similar position to you. If you have just moved to a new town it may help you to develop a social life.

3   **Involve yourself in departmental activities.** You don't have to occupy yourself with your research 100 per cent of the time. Make the time and effort to join in with other activities in the department whether these are social activities, guest lectures, open days for students, and so on. It will make your life more interesting and your participation will be appreciated by others in the department.

4   **Start some activities for postgraduates.** If there isn't a postgraduate society in your university or a researchers' group in your department then why not start one?

5   **Coffee breaks.** If there is a common room or dining room where you can go for a hot drink, or to eat at lunch time, make use of it. You might feel awkward at first because you don't know anyone but you soon will and you could otherwise find yourself stuck at your desk or bench all day not speaking to anyone.

6   **Share an office.** Sometimes it seems ideal to have an office to yourself, but it may be better to share with one or more people to ward off isolation (in many universities you may not get the choice anyway!).

7   **Cultivate kindred spirits.** Most research students make new friends with fellow-researchers. Such friendships often become lifelong ones, as there's a lot in common. It's really useful to have some friends who understand what the problems of research feel like.

8   **Don't forget to maintain contact with distant friends.** It's dangerously easy to get so busy researching that you don't get round to writing letters or ringing friends and family up. A phone call doesn't have to last hours, and it only takes a minute to write a short letter!

9   **Keep your interests going.** You may well find that your work takes a lot more time than when you were an undergraduate, but that doesn't mean you've got to give up favourite interests, hobbies or sports. You may just have to be a bit more careful rationing your time.

10 **Communicate electronically.** Many researchers have the opportunity to use e-mail, computer conferencing, and the World Wide Web. This can provide a way of making and maintaining contact with other people studying your topic, and keeping up with the news.

19

Recording and logging activity

1   **Keep duplicate records.** Make sure you have copies of any important or even possibly important records. It's useful to keep a complete set of anything important at each of two different places – one place could get burned down!

2   **Label everything.** That includes piles of questionnaires and interview transcripts, cassette tapes, printouts of data and so on. You really can forget what they are and spend a long time trying to identify them. It's well worth putting dates on them all as well.

3   **Keep track of your computer files.** Make sure that everything is labelled on the computer not just on hard copy print outs, otherwise it can be very hard to identify a 'wanted' file at a later stage. If you have problems remembering the peculiar file names you call files, make sure that the filename is printed on hard copies (for example in a page footer).

4   **Keep a log or diary.** You'll never be able to imagine that you could forget what you did and when – but you will! Then when you want to write 'data was collected from x, y, z, between such and such dates', you'll be in difficulties. Keep your activity logged. A small hardbacked book may be more durable and more portable (but also more-easily lost!) than loose leaf files. You may end up with a number of such books.

5   **Log the incidental.** There may be contextual events or activities which may affect your data, whether it be climatic conditions, a general election underway at the time, the opening of a new by-pass. Keep a note of everything.

6   **Experiment with formats for logging things.** You could use a diary, a pro-forma you design yourself, a plain notebook, index cards, a computer database and so on. Find out what works for you and whether you may need more than one kind of record for different things.

7   **Label drafts.** When you are writing something up label drafts and different versions. It's very easy to confuse old and new versions. If you are using a word processor you can usually get the date automatically printed out.

8   **Save successive drafts separately.** Computer space is not expensive. Rather than continuing to save successive versions of a paper under the original file name, it's better to save each major change as a new version. This means you can (for example) go back and retrieve the wonderful sentence that you've had second thoughts about since you deleted it!

9   **Files, not piles!** You'll be surprised how quickly you accumulate paperwork. You'll save a lot of time in the long run if you establish a filing system for it all. If you're lucky enough to have part or all of a filing cabinet, make good use of it. If not, it doesn't cost too much to buy some box files and some document wallets, and with these you can soon establish a sensible way of differentiating and storing papers, handouts, data, photocopies of articles, and so on.

10   **Somewhere, keep track of how you** *feel*. This could be in a personal diary or log book, or in a computer file. You may in future years find it useful to be able to tell future research students of the stages you went through as your research started, developed, and came to its successful conclusion.

20

Looking after yourself

One of the biggest differences between researching and being an under-graduate is that the timescales are much longer. You need to be able to maintain your momentum for longer stretches. The following suggestions should help you keep an appropriate balance.

1 **Pace yourself sensibly.** However much you feel under pressure to make rapid progress, don't set yourself a pace which you can't keep up comfortably for long periods of time.

2 **Remember you haven't got long vacations any more!** As an under-graduate, you may have been used to spells of intense work, with long periods to recover. As a researcher, your best plan is to avoid the need for recovery time.

3 **Eat sensibly.** Don't go for days without having food or replace it with booze! You need your body to be working for you, not against you.

4 **Get enough rest.** Sometimes if you're a bit stressed, sleep can be some-what elusive, but rest and relaxation is very beneficial in its own right. Remember that most people worry far too much. We often worry about things that we can't do anything about – this is pointless usually.

5 **Maintain a social life.** You may find you have less time for social activities than you had as an undergraduate, but this does not mean you're supposed to become a hermit. You may just have to ration your time a bit more strictly.

6 **Get some physical exercise.** Build in sensible regular exercise as part of your normal day, rather than as something you have to make spe-cial efforts to achieve. For example, walk part-way to and from the university rather than drive or use public transport all the way. A good workout on the squash court or a hike on a bike may be even better if you like such activities and are fit enough.

7   **Confront your own feelings.** Ask yourself regularly 'how do I feel today?'. If you find that your feelings are tending towards being over-stressed, it may be time to make some adjustments to your balance between work and the rest of your life.

8   **Build up your support network.** It can be really useful to have a few people you can lean on a little at times when things are getting you down. However, people don't like being leant on all the time – it gets boring! Make sure you're doing at least as much supporting of other people.

9   **Don't fight adversity too hard.** For example, if you have a bad dose of the 'flu, don't struggle on and try to work through it. It could take you a lot longer to get over it, and people you infected wouldn't thank you much for it!

10 **You can still have holidays!** They may be somewhat shorter than vacations used to be, but even a week off doing things you really enjoy can set you up to carry on the good work.

Chapter 3 Reading, Writing – And Finishing

This chapter is essentially about the principal milestones in doing research, especially for a higher degree. We start with four sets of suggestions about something you'll be doing a lot of – reading. It's important to pay attention to the quality of your reading, as otherwise the sheer quantity of things you read could become unmanageable; that's why we've included some tips about how to 'stop reading!'.

We move on next to your writing. If you're heading for a higher degree, putting together your thesis or dissertation is obviously one of the most important aspects of researching. Even if you're not heading for a higher degree, it's likely that you'll be required to write up your findings in some way – a report for example. We suggest that you start writing very early. You can always improve what you write, maybe many times before the final version.

We look next at conferences. Going to conferences may be a new experience for you, and it can be a very rewarding (and very enjoyable) part of the life of a researcher, as well as providing excellent opportunities to network. We're assuming you're not going to be a passive delegate for long, so we include ideas about giving your first conference paper – and handling the somewhat daunting task of facing questions from a knowledgeable audience! This leads on to some ideas about getting your work published.

We continue with some thoughts about writing a 'transfer document', often required of research students who have initially registered for a Masters degree, but who are moving straight on towards a PhD registration.

We end this chapter by looking at the final stages in your writing – putting together your thesis, and preparing for and giving a viva for a higher degree. In practice, the sooner you start thinking about all this the better; when you're heading in this direction the time goes surprisingly quickly. We've not tried to provide advice about the tone and style of your writing, as the requirements and traditions for this vary enormously from one discipline to another. We have, however, included some suggestions which apply to all disciplines – not least where we've seen problems arise when people don't seem to have been aware of the expectations of examiners.

21

Literature searches

Academic research must show that it is based on a knowledge of previous relevant work and awareness of the relevant theories, debates and controversies. Get on top of referencing conventions now!

1   **Start with your supervisors.** They should be able to point you to the key texts, articles and authors in the field. This will give you a starting point in becoming familiar with the subject and help you to define what other kinds of literature you need to access.

2   **Contact a librarian.** These people are the experts in how to do a literature search and it is their job to help people like you. Take time to talk to them about what you're trying to do, and ask for the benefit of their experience in the field.

3   **Find out which are the relevant abstracting and indexing services and computer databases for your topic.** These services are ways of finding articles, books and reports on specific topics but each one only covers a particular subject eg Chemical Abstracts or ERIC, the educational database. You may need more than one source especially if yours is an inter-disciplinary topic.

4   **Define your subject.** To carry out a literature search you need to know what you are searching for as well as where to search. Mostly you search by key words which define your topic, but it may not be easy to find the right keywords and some trial and error may be involved. Don't simply stick to the words you think of first. Consider how else the topic might be expressed and try alternatives.

5   **Play with combinations of key words.** Keyword 'X' might yield 104 references in a search, and keyword 'Y' a further 73 references. Keywords 'X' and 'Y' together may yield only nine references, which may well be the most important ones for you in the first place.

6   **Consider date and place.** In some subjects you find that a huge amount has been published. But is it all relevant? One way of cutting down is to consider the date of publication. For example, would you consider material more than 20 years old or 10 years old to be relevant to your research? Is it the UK situation only which is of interest to you, if so will research based on experience in the USA, Japan, West Africa, or Italy be of interest?

7   **Be systematic.** Always keep records of where you have searched (so that you don't have to do it again), how you searched ie which key words you used, and of course keep a careful record of what you found. This means a full list of the items with their full references. This saves a great deal of time and energy when it comes to writing the bibliography in your thesis.

8   **Update yourself.** From your initial literature search you will identify where research of interest to you is usually published. You should then arrange to scan the relevant journals or reports as they come out so that you keep right up to date. Carry on searching, and keep your reference bank updated.

9   **But there isn't anything!** It may indeed be true that little or nothing has been written on your research topic. However, first of all check that you have searched thoroughly, in all the right places and using the correct approach. After that you may need to think laterally investigating related topics and disciplines. Apart from showing that you have used some relevant literature, other people's ideas and views are always useful. You need them to help your research along.

10   **Keep 'quotes' as well as publication details.** When you find an important reference, it is never too early to capture words you may wish to quote from them in your final thesis or dissertation. Having carefully transcribed quotes to hand can save you having to look up the references all over again.

22

Keeping track of the literature

When researching, it's important not only to keep abreast of the literature in your field, but also to keep track of what you read, so that you will be able to provide comprehensive and accurate records when you compile your thesis or dissertation. The following suggestions should help you do both.

1   **Design a system to store references.** Most researchers build up a card index to keep data about important references. It is also possible to build up your data on references on computer.

2   **Find out 'who's who?' in your field.** This is not always easy to start with, but your supervisor should be able to give you good advice. Going to subject conferences is often a good way of finding out more about who's doing what in your field. Once you have the names of important contributors to the field, it's much easier to watch out for new publications from them as new issues of journal are published.

3   **Get to know the most important journals in your field.** Your supervisor will have a good idea about the journals to keep track of, but always be on the lookout for other sources as well. Once you've identified the main journals to follow, keep track of them regularly.

4   **Make an 'important journal' checklist.** Write down the names of the main journals in your field, and the dates of publication of recent and forthcoming issues. Tick off when you've seen each issue and searched it for articles relevant to your studies. This avoids the possibility of missing an important new contribution to your field.

5   **Keep accurate records of important articles.** Whether using card indexes or a computer database, record the details of each article in exactly the same way as you may wish to reference it in your dissertation. For example:
Bloggs, J and Podsworthy, A (1996) *The effects of temperature on research efficiency*, J Research Processes, 4, 21–9.

6   **Keep accurate records of articles or chapters in books.** Use your card index (or computer database) to keep these references in the form which you may use in future to quote them in your thesis or dissertation. For example:
Bloggs, J (1996) 'The effects of humidity on research efficiency' in *A New Perspective of the Effects of Everything on Research* edited by Podsworthy, A Acme Books, London and West Bromwich, UK.

7   **See if other people can work with you.** When you're working in a field which overlaps with work done by fellow-researchers, you can take some of the drudgery out of searching the literature by splitting the journals you'll scan, and scanning for each other's topics.

8   **Take photocopies of important articles.** This doesn't mean everything! Don't take the view 'I'll photocopy it in case it may be important' – this would be a cop-out (and expensive) regarding your task of deciding what's important as and when you read it. In any case, if you're keeping data on good references, you can always go back to an article which turns out to be important, and make a copy of it at a later stage – if you've got a good record of the article in your database or card index.

9   **Use search facilities available in your library.** This is particularly useful when you've already got the names of key contributors to the field, as well as when you've identified the topic keywords which are worth searching for in the field.

10   **Plan in time to attend to your literature database.** It's all too easy to say 'I'll do this next week when I've more time'! When research gets exciting, it is tempting to shelve work on your literature database collection 'till later', but it's well worth getting into the discipline of spending at least half a day each week entirely devoted to keeping up with the literature.

23

Getting the most from your librarians

Librarians can help you a lot. They can guide you through a basic literature search or even do it for you, help you to keep up to date with the latest publications, find some particular facts or statistics which you need, suggest avenues for publication – and much more!

1 **Start at the beginning.** Contact your librarians at the beginning of your research so you benefit from their help and they are pleased that you have come to them first. Librarians really like to feel they're being useful.

2 **Don't underestimate librarians!** Many subject librarians have degrees and higher degrees, and know what it's like to do research. They may have a lot of knowledge about the broad field you're researching in, and may know (for example) the relative reputations of many published researchers in the field.

3 **If at first you don't succeed. . .** Most librarians want to help the library users – it is their job to serve. However, if you should encounter one who isn't helpful, try someone else. Most academic libraries have a large enough library staff for you to be able to do this.

4 **Never be afraid to ask for help.** Just because you're now a researcher doesn't mean that you're expected to be entirely self-sufficient when it comes to tracking down the most relevant literature in your topic.

5 **Make appointments.** Believe it or not librarians are busy people. Don't expect them to be able to spend all afternoon helping you at the drop of a hat. If possible call in and make an appointment, or if there is no such system, go into the library at a quiet time, for example, not over lunch time when the library is full to bursting with undergraduate students and half the staff are away eating their lunch.

6   **Stick to the rules.** Show you are responsible and trustworthy. For example if you're allowed a special loan of a book, take care of it and return it on time. Librarians like people who stick to the rules, not because they are naturally authoritarian but because they're the ones who get the complaints when other library users are inconvenienced.

7   **Voice your appreciation.** Librarians are only human and they like a 'thank you' from time to time. If your librarian has been particularly helpful why not put your thanks in writing? Or a pint?

8   **Be honest about your ignorance.** If you don't know anything about using libraries and literature searching and can't tell an abstract from an abscess – say so! Don't try to pretend – you'll be caught out, and it's better to have the librarians on your side and trying to help you.

9   **Don't expect miracles.** Librarians know about the technicalities of literature searching such as where you should search for your topic, and will probably have some good suggestions about synonyms and ways of describing the topic but they don't know your subject in detail. They probably can't tell you which ones of the 105 apparently relevant references are really key to your research. You will have to use your own judgment.

10   **Use library networks.** Librarians can put you in touch with other libraries and information services if you need them. Nowadays a lot of material is available via inter-library loan which cuts down on the need to visit other libraries except to browse in specialised collections or access rare materials which you might need if you are studying some aspects of literature or history.

24

Stop reading!

You remember the expression 'reading for a degree'. Now you may be reading for a higher degree. That's an awful lot of reading! The danger is that reading can so easily swallow up all of your time – there's usually so much to read. You may need to adjust your approach to reading in general. Here are our ideas on this.

1   **Develop your powers of scanning.** Practise finding out what an article or a book chapter is about without actually reading it. Look at headings and subheadings, glance at illustrations and figures, and find out enough about the material to help you make a sensible decision regarding whether you should really read it.

2   **Make good use of contents pages and indexes in journals and books.** These can help you track down relevant articles and passages much faster than working your way through everything that has a relevant looking title. Many journals publish an author and/or keyword index once a year – check when this happens for the journals closest to your research area.

3   **You can read much faster than you speak!** Surprisingly many people allow themselves to be trapped by the way they learned to read at school, vocalising words as they went. Practice reading deliberately fast, taking in clusters of words, and letting your brain gather the general sense linking them up.

4   **Find out whose work to read seriously.** This takes a bit of patience, but if you keep your eyes and ears open you'll soon find out from other people who they think the principal authors worth following are.

5   **Identify things you're going to read in detail.** Make careful notes of the sources and bibliographic details of passages or papers that you will want to refer to in your work.

6 **Take photocopies of important short articles or extracts.** Carry some of these (not all of them!) around with you wherever you go. You can do some useful reading almost anywhere, and this can be a painless way of helping to avoid reading interfering with your research activities.

7 **When reading important material, mark up your photocopies (or books and journals you own).** This can save you a lot of time when you come to consult them further. You may also like to store main details systematically in a card file, or on a computer database (but back up either – losing such things can be a disaster!).

8 **Make use of what others have read.** Many book chapters and journal articles include a review of existing research work in the field. These can be a valuable source of references for your own work, and you may not need to read the originals in detail to get the gist of them – which will often be nicely captured in the reviews.

9 **Make full use of abstracts collections.** A photocopy of a short abstract may be all you need to store the bibliographic details and main points of an article or even a book.

10 **Build up your personal list of relevant keywords.** Use this in doing bibliographic searches, and when using the indexes of journals and books. Remember to do retrospective searches of material you've already scanned, when you add important new topic keywords to your agenda.

25

Starting your writing

In the long term, writing your thesis or dissertation is probably the most important thing you'll do when working towards a higher degree. Even if you're not going in for a higher degree, research reports will be a major part of your work. Like any big task, it can become only too easy to find yourself postponing the start of writing. The following suggestions should help you get going – and keep going.

1 **Start early.** It's a really big mistake to do your research and leave all your writing until the end. Writing should be an integral part of your research right from the outset.

2 **Ask yourself the key questions.** Try and find the key questions you need answer such as: 'Why am I doing what I'm doing?', 'What has been done before?', 'Why am I doing it differently?', 'What are the key problems?', and so on. Use the key questions to start you off writing.

3 **Start writing under these headings.** Use the questions to structure your writing. Think of new headings to go with each idea you feel like writing about. You will find it a lot easier, later, to arrange your headings into the most sensible order, than it would be to arrange unheaded paragraphs or pages into the best sequence.

4 **Don't be a perfectionist in the early stages.** Recognise that it is more important to make a start on writing rather than getting it absolutely right first time. Besides, it's much easier for you to feel relaxed about making changes and improvements if you haven't set your mind on having got your existing bits and pieces 'perfect'.

5 **Work on a word processor from the start.** You will certainly want to draft and redraft your work, so it's wasteful to pay for it to be typed and retyped. Get straight onto a machine yourself. You'll probably be surprised how quickly your typing skills improve.

6   **Take a typing course if you need it.** You don't have to attend a live course, there are many computer-based programmes which give you structured practise in typing, and help you develop your speed. It's really worth learning to use all of your fingers, with the aim of eventually becoming able to touch-type. When you can touch-type much faster than you handwrite, you'll be glad you persisted. Twenty minutes every day for three weeks will do it!

7   **Don't worry about spelling mistakes or 'typos'.** It's best to go with the flow of your ideas, and get them down quickly if roughly. You can use spellchecks later to sort out the mistakes.

8   **Keep multiple copies of everything.** Save your writing every few minutes – don't be caught out losing a couple of hours work when there's a power cut (we've all done this *once!*). Back up your discs and back up your back ups. Keep paper copies too in case there are problems with machines.

9   **Keep your work secure.** Don't keep all your material on one machine with the back up discs beside it. Thefts, floods and fires do happen! Keep a complete set of your discs both at work and at home. Hard discs and floppies can fail, so minimise the risks, and keep one copy of your work on hard disc anyway.

10 **Get feedback on your bits of writing.** Ask colleagues and supervisors to scribble on printouts of your work as it develops. Edit and improve your work on disc straightaway, before you have the chance to forget what their comments are.

26

Structuring your writing

Writing a thesis or dissertation is a much bigger job that writing up a project. However, many of the same principles continue to apply. The following suggestions should help you organise your writing efficiently and as painlessly as possible.

1 **Make a visual plan of the whole thesis.** It helps to be able to keep a running check on progress with the whole thing. Use a large sheet of paper, for example a flipchart sheet. Put your thesis title in a box towards the centre of the sheet, and scatter round the outside of the sheet the titles of your successive chapters. There are some computer packages which help you to do this and allow you to keep checking and developing your plan as new inspirations occur. Share your plan with your supervisor and others.

2 **Get a set of different coloured document wallets.** Reserve one for each chapter of your thesis or dissertation. As you gradually accumulate bits and pieces that will end up in the respective chapters, store them in the wallets. You may also choose to get a box file, to keep the whole set of wallets safely. Remember, though, to have at least one other copy of everything important somewhere else too.

3 **Keep an eye on the relationships between chapters.** Use your visual plan to check that you're structuring the chapters in the most sensible order.

4 **Make sensible decisions about appendices.** The purpose of appendices is to contain information which needs to be present in your thesis, but which would interrupt the flow and impact of your chapters if you were to present it straight away. Don't have appendices just for the sake of having them – all should be relevant and necessary in some way.

5   **Take your time to get the introduction right.** There's no second chance to make a good first impression. People reading your work will make important assumptions about the quality of your work soon after they start reading it; try to ensure that these assumptions will be favourable. Make sure the thesis will start with a clear explanation of the purpose or rationale of your work. Allow for the fact that plans may change as work develops. Within reason, feel free to adjust and amend your rationale on the basis of what actually happens during your work. Revisit your rationale objectively when you're coming to the end of your work.

6   **Make a short, careful summary to add to the end of each chapter.** It's worth starting these in draft form along with the earliest drafts of the chapters, so that by the time the finished version is printed there has been ample opportunity for you to refine and polish the summaries.

7   **Take particular care with your final chapter.** A good thesis ends strongly – not with a whimper. For example, you may wish to give a concise review of the whole of your work, and an account of suggestions for further relevant research work.

8   **Make a really good abstract.** Probably abstracts are best when they are less than a page in length. Many more people may read your abstract than those who will consult your text in detail. The abstract should give a concise but accurate picture of what your thesis is about. Your abstract will probably be published separately in its own right in collections of abstracts, and needs to be as self-explanatory as possible.

9   **Be really careful about your bibliography.** Double-check that every reference cited in your text is listed correctly in your bibliography. Also double-check that you haven't left references in your bibliography which you have not referred to in your text (for example when you've discarded part of a chapter).

10   **Find a good proof reader.** Be prepared to pay for this if necessary.

27

Graphs, illustrations and diagrams

Most theses contain a fair number of such things. They can make all the difference to your words – 'a picture can be worth a thousand words'! However, it's easier to get the words right than it is to make the illustrations right – the following suggestions may help you achieve both.

1   **Have a clear purpose for each illustration.** Think how it will in due course help your reader to make sense of your findings.

2   **Make each illustration as self-explanatory as possible.** Aim towards each graph, illustration or diagram needing no reference to the text of your writing to make its purpose clear.

3   **Make your illustrations look professional.** It's worth learning to use a package that generates good graphs, diagrams, pie-charts, histograms, and so on. Alternatively, it's not hard these days to find a student who can do these things for you. Check up with people around you which desktop publishing packages are most suitable for the sorts of illustrations you wish to use. Look for packages where you have good control of lettering both on the illustrations themselves and for captions.

4   **Take particular care with caption numbering.** Make sure that the numbers correlate with the section headings of your thesis. Also, double check that you don't get the figure numbers out of synch. with their references in your text, especially when you decide to insert an additional figure somewhere. Check also that the print sizes and fonts will be consistent for all of your figures. Likewise, if you're using figure headings, make sure that the way you use these is consistent throughout your work.

5   **Check carefully the exact positioning of your illustrations.** Try to ensure that when a figure is referred to in your text, it will be visible to the reader immediately. It is useful to include in your draft manuscripts 'Figure X about here please'. This is also useful practice for future journal articles and papers.

6   **Check carefully that the axes on graphs are fully labelled.** Each axis should state what is being plotted, and the dimensions in which the graph is made. Also ensure that tables of data are provided, maybe in an appendix, for all important graphs. Make sure that tables are fully labelled too, and refer correctly to the illustrations based on them.

7   **Make sure that illustrations will appear 'big enough'.** It is all too easy to allow figures to appear so compressed that readers will not be able to make sense of all the information in their labelling and captions. Be particularly careful that subscripts and superscripts are large enough to be read clearly.

8   **Prepare for the 'list of figures'.** Any good thesis contains such an element. This should turn out to be an effective index to the illustrations you use. Probably the safest way to compile the list of figures is by collecting together on wordprocessor the exact captions along with the figure numbers. Using a particular font or print style just for figure captions can make it possible collect them all together very simply with many wordprocessing packages – just by deleting everything else! (But take care not to accidentally lose your text – always keep backup copies).

9   **Keep paper copies of your original illustrations.** This is especially important when you cut and paste them into a wordprocessing package. You'll need your original artwork if you submit your work to a journal, and you may well want to make transparencies or slides of some of your figures.

10   **Get someone else to check your figures before your thesis is bound!** It often takes someone else's eyes to notice a hiccup in the numbering, or an incorrect text reference to an illustration. If you're using (or buying) a proof reader, ask for special attention to your illustrations and the way they are referred to in your text.

28

Attending conferences

When you're just starting research, the first conference you attend can be daunting. Everyone seems to know so much more than you do! However, there is much that can be gained from a conference. We hope the following suggestions give you some ideas.

1 **Read the pre-conference documentation well.** Look for who's doing what. Look out for names you've already come across in the literature. Ask people around you. Your supervisor (or fellow-researchers) may be able to help you plan what you want to concentrate on at the conference. Ask who they know, and who they've heard of or read about. Look for sessions which seem close to your research field or topic, and mark up the conference documentation to remind you of which sessions you plan to attend – sometimes there will be very little time between sessions and you won't have time to make wise choices at the last moment.

2 **Don't feel you have to attend every session and take in everything.** With the best intentions in the world, you'll only really remember the occasional part of it a few weeks later.

3 **Don't worry when some sessions are right over your head.** They're often over everyone else's head as well, but people tend to nod and look as though they understand everything.

4 **Make concise, clear notes.** Don't try to write down everything you see, hear or think! A few well-chosen words will be much easier to follow-up later. Write down questions in your notes. Write down things that you may want to find out more about later. Write down questions that other people seem to be keen on finding the answers to. When you have a good stock of questions, you're well on your way to most of the answers.

5   **Use conferences to tune in to how to write papers.** Look at the tone, style and presentation that presenters use in their conference papers and handouts. Look particularly at the ways they refer to published work.

6   **Make friends and contacts.** It's useful to identify some fellow-researchers in other institutions or colleges, and form the beginning of a mutual support network. Research can be lonely at times even in a busy department, when you're the only new researcher. A friendly voice at the end of a phone line can be very welcome.

7   **Use the coffee breaks, meals, and the bar!** Experienced conference-goers will confirm that the time outside sessions usually turns out to be the most valuable part of a conference.

8   **Make your own reflective log of the conference.** This particularly applies to conferences spanning two or more days. It's well worth-while sitting down for a few minutes at the end of each day, and just jotting down your own feelings, reactions, and thoughts.

9   **Go back to your own drafts.** Annotate your own work as soon as possible after a conference to bring your work right up to date, including references to relevant conference contributions and papers.

10   **Write up a short conference report immediately after the event.** Sometimes you may be required or expected to do this. In any case, writing a report is a very useful way of sorting out which parts of the conference were directly relevant to you.

29

Giving your first conference paper

You'll always remember your first! Even if you've given presentations before, it can be quite stressful talking in a formal way to established subject experts in your field. The following suggestions on preparing and delivering a conference paper should help you minimise the stress.

1   **Have your paper ready in plenty of time.** It would only add to the stress if you were in the position of still trying to complete your paper the week before the conference.

2   **Get advance feedback on your paper.** Ask fellow-research students to scribble all over a copy, and also ask your supervisor and anyone else who can give you useful feedback. It's usually worth making a further draft of your paper based on feedback comments. Rehearse presenting your paper to some of your faculty colleagues and ask for their suggestions.

3   **Find out how long your slot will be.** Conferences often fall behind schedule, so if you've got (for example) a 30-minute slot, start planning how you'll accommodate things if you end up with only 20 minutes.

4   **Plan to leave time for questions.** Conference audiences can feel quite cheated if you talk for all of your slot, and don't give delegates the chance to ask questions or make comments on your work.

5   **Be prepared for awkward questions!** Some delegates seem to delight in putting presenters on the spot. Try to anticipate as many as possible of the likely questions you may get, by asking fellow-researchers to jot down questions they think are possible.

6   **Turn your paper into a handout, and prepare sufficient copies.**
Sometimes, such material may be sent out by the conference organis-
ers in advance. If not, have your handout materials available on the
day.

7   **You don't have to present it all!** A handout gives you greater flexibility regarding what you talk about. When time is limited, or when you
don't want to elaborate much on a given part of your work, you can
refer your audience to the handout.

8   **Choose whether to give out your handout at the start of your session,
or at the end.** The choice depends on your style. If you prefer to read
out your paper more-or-less verbatim, it's best not to give copies out
till the end (people hate someone reading out to them something they
can read for themselves – and much faster!). But let your audience
know that you're going to give them a copy at the end – it's frustrat-
ing for them to spend energy making notes only to be given a printed
copy later.

9   **Prepare audio or visual support for your presentation.** For example
prepare overhead transparencies containing the main points you wish
to make, or the main questions you wish to address. Use one as early
as possible in your presentation – it takes the eyes off you for a while
as you get settled into your talk. Don't put too much on any one
transparency – people at the back need to be able to read them.

10   **Get your pile into order.** Mark up your script with clear indications of
when you wish to refer the audience to part of a handout, and when
to display each overhead. Make sure your overheads are in the right
order.

11   **Get off to a good start.** Start by saying a little about yourself (who you
are, where you're researching, what you're researching, and so on).
Then speak for a minute or so about the aims of this particular presentation.

12   **Pay attention to the way you deliver your paper.** Strike a balance
between reading from a script (which can be dreadfully dull!) or talking around a paper (which can be scary!).

13   **Keep track of the time.** Put your watch where you can see it while
you talk, without obviously looking at it all the time. Make a careful
note of the exact time at which you intend to have finished your
speaking, and plan to move over to discussion with the audience. It's
quite common for your actual presentation to take longer than when
you rehearsed it (but have a few extra things you can talk about
should the opposite happen!).

14   **Don't bluff!** You will be speaking to a knowledgeable audience so be honest about where you are in your research. If you have only completed the pilot study then say so! If you try to claim more the audience will probably spot this, and you may be in for some tough questions at the end of your presentation.

15   **Come to a solid conclusion before passing over to the audience for questions.** Don't just 'stop'. It's useful to conclude by summing up your main points 'in a nutshell', accompanied by an overhead transparency which says 'Conclusions' or 'Summary'. Such actions help the audience feel that your presentation is well structured.

16   **Repeat the questions.** This helps other people in the audience who may not have been able to hear the questions properly. It also gives you time to think! In addition, it is a chance to make sure that you've captured the essence of the question correctly before you start to address it – check your questioner's face for any signs that this is not so.

17   **Don't panic when asked questions where you don't know the answer.** Your audience will be much more patient if you're honest about this.

18   **Give opportunities to your questioners.** Sometimes people ask questions – often lengthy ones – because they themselves have something they want to say. However uncomfortable you feel if you can't respond to such questions, you can often pass the buck back to the questioner with words such as 'That sounds like an interesting approach. Could you say just a bit more about it, and how you see that it may relate to the work I have been describing?'.

19   **Check that you've answered questions (when you know you have!).** Look back at the questioner and ask 'Does this answer your question?'.

20   **Make the most of being a new researcher.** At this stage in your research you should not feel that you must be able to answer any question you're asked. People will happily accept a response along the lines 'That hasn't arisen in my research yet' – 'I'm only at the early stages' or 'I hadn't considered this, but now I will do'.

30

Getting started in publishing

Reputations are not just built on the quality of research work, but on the printed words which tell the world what you've done. The sooner you start publishing the better. The following suggestions may help you start.

1   **Target your market**. Some journals are easier than others regarding getting published as a new author. Ask experienced colleagues in your field where it may be best to start. Find out which journals or periodicals have the highest standing in your subject area – you may be wise to avoid these until your own standing is high! Also check out how long it takes to get things into print – sometimes you may wish to go for a less austere journal for the sake of speed.

2   **Read the 'guidelines for authors'**. Most book publishers, journal and magazine editors and commissioners will have produced author guidelines which will help you get it right the first time. Stick to these guidelines religiously! Editors are usually very strict regarding such guidelines – it's easier to reject your article if all the other submissions conform to the rules and yours doesn't! Expect to draft and redraft a number of times. Wherever you are publishing, you will need to provide work that has been checked and polished.

3   **Seek out opportunities to publish.** Give the editors of likely journals a ring, and ask them if they may be interested in an article on such-and-such. They may give you useful suggestions regarding exactly what sort of material they are most keen to receive, and you may be able to tune in your work in the light of these suggestions.

4   **Conferences can be good!** If you can get a paper accepted at a conference, this may well get your work published in the conference proceedings. Some conferences publish all papers submitted, others use a preferred selection. Investigate this and make decisions accordingly. The same research can probably support two or three levels of publications such as a conference paper, a journal article and a section in a book.

5   **Take opportunities for joint publications.** Co-publishing with your supervisor is usually an excellent step towards publishing independently later.

6   **Check who owns your research.** Make sure that your research contract entitles you to publish results from your work. There may be constraints concerning ownership and timing.

7   **Check your tone and style.** Make sure that your writing is right for the context. You can gauge this by reading sample material in the field in which you are aiming to publish, and particularly articles in the particular journal you may be targeting.

8   **Take referees' comments seriously.** Normally, published material has to be agreed by one or more referees, chosen by the journal editor for their knowledge of the field. Referees are excellent sources of authoritative advice – and they're free! Established authors expect to learn a lot from referees' comments. Disagreeing with suggestions made by referees is not a sensible thing to do if you want to be published!

9   **Be prepared to shorten your work.** Journal editors often want to shorten articles, so that the journal can accommodate more contributions. If your style is too wordy, you may be asked to make cuts. Painful as it is to remove much loved paragraphs you have composed with care, it will probably improve your publication.

10 **Don't give up the first time an article is rejected.** You may be able to adapt it further and get it accepted later, or you may be able to get it published just as it is somewhere else. Don't allow yourself to be discouraged by rejections – every established author has had these – and most still get them!

31
Writing a transfer document

Many research students start off registering on a Masters programme, and after a year or so (providing their research is progressing successfully) can apply to transfer their registration to that for a PhD. Universities sometimes require such students to submit a 'transfer document' at this stage, and to have a viva to confirm that the transfer is appropriate. If you're ever going to be in this position, we hope the following suggestions will be helpful at this stage.

1 **Keep a positive attitude.** The transfer document may be the first major thing you've written since your final year degree dissertation. Take the opportunity as a practice run for the skeleton of your PhD thesis. More importantly, use this chance to take stock of your research work to date, and firm up what you are about to embark on. Don't regard writing your transfer document as a chore.

2 **Start writing in good time.** There will almost certainly be a firm deadline for submitting a transfer document. Write early, so you've got maximum chance to get feedback from other people – and for second thoughts. Judge how long to spend on it. Taking too long could eat into research time, and doing it too quickly brings the risk of making rash decisions.

3 **Don't do it alone.** Get advice from your supervisor. This is a time for maximum contact with your supervisor as you're about to make important decisions about the final stage of your PhD. Wrong decisions here could lead to a lot of time being wasted. Don't think of it as a chore.

4 **Obtain several copies of other people's transfer documents.** Look for examples in your subject and in your department. Ask your head of department what's considered to be an ideal transfer document. Compare with comments from your supervisor.

5 **Think about the order.** Don't necessarily write things in the order in which you carried out your work. It is supposed to be a summary of what you've already done, with clear reasons why your further studies are to be undertaken.

6 **Do a literature survey as you go along.** It saves a lot of time to have all the relevant references to hand, and to know which will be required in your transfer document.

7 **Don't put in too much experimental detail.** Probably the most important thing to get across is what you're intending to do for your PhD and why, and not how you did what you've already done.

8 **Get at least two other people to proof-read your document.** Ensure that at least one of your proof-readers has experience of what's expected in a transfer document.

9 **Write a clear abstract.** Remember that people reading your transfer document may not necessarily be experts in your specific area, even though they have a general knowledge of your subject. Make the abstract readable and interesting, leading gently into your proposed work.

10 **Put the bound copies in a drawer for a fortnight!** This gives you the opportunity to come back to it afresh, and read it in a way where you can spot the kind of points which may be focused on in your forthcoming interview or viva.

32

Selecting your examiner

For most higher degrees you will have two or more examiners who will read your thesis and discuss it with you at your viva. These examiners are appointed shortly before you are ready to submit, and there will usually be at least one internal examiner from the university where you're researching, and one external examiner from another university or research institution. You may be able to make suggestions about who your examiners should be. You need to know the procedures that your university uses.

1   **External examiners are often people well known by your supervisor.** This is usually an advantage, as your supervisor should then also know how qualified in your subject area the external is to examine your work. It does not, however, mean that the external examination will be a walkover!

2   **External examiners need to have a proven track record in your subject discipline.** This means in practice that your external examiner is highly likely to be someone who has published fairly extensively in a field close to your topic. Almost certainly, it will be someone whose work you've referenced in your thesis (all the more reasons to make sure these references are *absolutely* correctly listed, and that you've interpreted them quite correctly!).

3   **Most external examiners are chosen because they've been external examiners before!** Of course, there always has to be a first time. But if you're hoping to secure a particular external examiner (maybe someone whom you've already encountered at a conference, perhaps) the people responsible for authorising the choice will be more likely to accept such a person if there's already a record of external examining experience.

4   **Sometimes external examiners can end up being people whose work you've argued with!** If there has been some controversy regarding research findings, one way out is to get the protagonists together – this is not likely to be the most comfortable of external examining solutions!

5   **External examiners need to be available.** They're often distinguished people, and may be on another continent for periods of time. This can mean that you just can't always have the external examiner you'd really like, or even the one who is best qualified to examine your work.

6   **External examiners are not brilliantly paid.** Some may be in high demand for more lucrative consultancy or professional skills. This too can mean that the person you'd ideally like may well not be willing to take on external examining duties.

7   **If there's doubt about your work, a tough external examiner may be chosen!** Universities have to protect the perceived standards of their higher degrees, and your supervisor's hand may be forced if it is believed that your work should be given a particular thorough going over.

8   **Sometimes, the only possibility for an external examiner will be someone no-one knows.** This is likely to be the case if your research is in a very specialised field, when there's no-one other than a particular expert to draw on. If this happens, it may pay to do some last-post literature searching, and to accommodate comments on published work from this person.

9   **Avoid compromise.** This may seem obvious, but it's important that no-one could accuse you of engineering things so that someone you knew quite well ended up as your external examiner.

10   **Don't forget internal examiners!** It's not unknown for internal examiners to be tougher than the external. Find out as much as you can about your internal examiner, and prepare accordingly!

33

Submitting your thesis

We've given lots of suggestions in various parts of this book about the preparation of your thesis. This set is intended as a final checklist, for use in the days leading up to the actual submission of your work.

1   **Check how many copies you'll need.** There may be a minimum number, including a copy each for your external examiner, the university library, your department, and perhaps your supervisor. You may well wish to prepare one or more additional copies – not least to ensure that you retain one yourself! It's usually cheaper to get all the copies you'll need printed and bound at the same time.

2   **Check carefully the rules about binding, lettering and format.** Theses (certainly PhD ones) normally have to conform strictly to format, so they will appear in a standard form in the university library. Look at several recent examples to check exactly how the wording should appear on the front cover and on the spine.

3   **Check the normal internal format for theses.** See what the normal relative order of such things as abstract, acknowledgements, contents pages, main body of work, bibliography and appendices are, and see whether the preceding odds-and-ends are numbered 'i-xii' and so on, with the thesis itself starting at '1'.

4   **Don't forget your acknowledgements!** Some people will expect to be mentioned, and for others it could be a really nice courtesy to do so. It's worth reading the acknowledgements pages of a dozen theses just to check the sorts of people that normally get mentioned, and the acceptable ways of thanking them.

5   **Make a very clear copy of the exact wording you require on your front cover and spine.** You'll normally be passing this over to the binders, and it would be very embarrassing if words or spellings were wrong on your final thesis copies, for example if your writing was difficult to read.

6   **Make use of your final chance to check for errors.** You won't feel like doing this, but it's worth it. If you do find errors at this late stage, it's still not impossible to get replacement copies of any pages that are affected printed quickly.

7   **If you're required to sort out your sheafs of paper into sets, do this carefully!** It's easy to end up with one set containing page 47 twice, and one (always the copy destined for the external examiner) containing no such page!

8   **If possible, keep for yourself one copy of the printout.** It's very nervewracking passing over your work for binding, and having a 'rescue' position is well worth the comfort it gives. Binding seems as though it takes for ever!

9   **Be clear about exactly where to submit your copies, and by what date.** It could be unfortunate if you took them all to the wrong place at the last minute, and then found that the right place had just closed for the week!

10   **Even after your copies are 'in the system' and out of your control, keep checking.** There could still be errors or omissions. It's better to come along to your viva with an errata list and your apologies than to hope that no-one will have spotted any defects – someone always has.

34

Preparing for your viva

If you're going in for a research degree, your viva will be an important day. It can also seem a very stressful ordeal! The following preparations should help you to maximise your chances of success, and minimise the anxiety.

1   **Talk to other people who've had vivas.** Ask them what went well, and what went badly. Build up your own picture of the sort of general questions which are asked at most vivas. Ask people how they'd approach it differently if they were going to do it again.

2   **Remind yourself what the viva is for.** Vivas are used to ensure that candidates' work is indeed their own, as well as to authenticate the validity of research work.

3   **Find out who will be there.** For example, there could be an external examiner, an internal examiner, and your supervisor may be present too (but usually not as an examiner as such, but to give some support if you need it).

4   **Find out about the external examiner.** Such people are normally chosen because they've done research work themselves in your field. Look up their references, and make sure their work is duly referred to in your thesis (positively, not too critically!). Don't keep examiners waiting for your thesis. If examiners get it only a day before your viva, they're not likely to be well-disposed at the need to find time in a busy schedule to read it properly.

5   **Work out some of the questions you may be asked.** Your examiners' questions will mostly be based very much on the words you've written in your thesis. Read it through again and again, so that you're very familiar exactly where you wrote what. Get friends to give you mock vivas. Practising for the big day with fellow-research students can be mutually productive, and can spare you from nasty surprise questions. Rehearse your answers to likely questions. The acts of putting your explanations into words, and speaking these words to fellow students, help you to come across more calmly and convincingly on the actual day.

6   **Identify for yourself any errors in your thesis.** Of course, in this book we've been trying to make sure that you don't have any errors, be they typographical, factual, or in the bibliography. That said, there will probably still be one or two which have slipped through despite everything. It looks much better at your viva if you are seen to have noticed them yourself.

7   **See if your supervisor is willing to give you a dry run.** The more practised you get at handling questions about your work, the more confident you should become. Remember that your supervisor may well be 'tougher' than your real examiners, due to knowing all the more about the actual development of your work.

8   **Expect to have to make revisions.** Don't go into your viva thinking that the first thing that is found wrong means that you are doomed! It is perfectly normal to have corrections, additions and clarifications to attend to after a viva.

9   **Prepare to be mentally alert.** Build in time for rest and/or exercise before your viva.

10 **Remember that examiners are still human beings.** They're probably going to want you to succeed. And if you haven't yet succeeded, they will probably want to point you in the right direction so that you will succeed soon.

35

Giving your viva

As we've already mentioned in this book, the viva you give for a research degree can be an important and memorable day in your life. There are several things you can do (and avoid doing) once in the viva room to make things better. Here are our ideas.

1   **Prepare to be at ease!** Be early. Stay overnight somewhere close if significant travel is involved. Plan not to have to rush off afterwards – it's hard to estimate how long a viva may take. Most seem to last a couple of hours, sometimes with lunch in the middle. Choose what to wear. It's usually better to be fairly formal rather than to find yourself underdressed – if things become more relaxed than you expected you can shed a jacket or tie.

2   **Get off to a comfortable start.** Greet your examiners appropriately. They will normally try to put you at ease by introducing themselves and shaking hands with you shortly after you're summoned to their presence! Don't sit in the wrong chair! Your examiners will normally have worked out where they want to sit, and how they want to structure the interview. Wait to be motioned to where they intend you to be.

3   **Don't expect it to be a walkover.** Your examiners (the external one at least) are being paid for examining you, and will have prepared some questions, comments and criticisms simply to justify being there, however good your work is.

4   **Don't expect it to be a disaster.** Some vivas may be unsuccessful, but there are almost always opportunities to redeem the situation by making corrections to your work, doing some additional work, or even rewriting substantial parts of it.

5   **Don't not speak!** It is very difficult to keep a viva going if the candidate just gives short answers such as 'yes' and 'no' to each successive question. In fact, the more you manage to do the talking, the less awkward silences there will be, and the better everyone (including you) will feel you are doing.

6   **Keep going when you're winning!** When you're talking about part of your work you're really confident about, try to make sure that you keep the floor for a while at least.

7   **Don't interrupt your examiners.** If they've heard enough from you about the bit you're really enjoying talking about, take the hint when they want to move you on to another question.

8   **Don't go on the defensive.** Some of their comments will be critical. Listen carefully to this feedback. It will often be very useful information regarding making your thesis better, or even making adjustments when preparing parts of your work for future publication. Remember that if anything goes badly wrong you may be entitled to appeal against the decision reached at your viva – but don't start appealing before you know that you need to!

9   **Be ready for 'are there any questions you would like to ask us?'** Don't ask 'Have I passed then?' (The examiners normally have to have at least a few minutes of private discussion to confirm that you've passed – and attend to the associated paperwork). Have something relevant to ask – something perhaps that you know your external examiner will be pleased to talk about!

10 **Thank your examiners for their time and attention.** This is a much better way to finish your big day than just diving out of the door at the first opportunity – however much you're tempted!

Chapter 4 Getting Going With Teaching

Most researchers find themselves involved in teaching in one way or another. Sometimes it's part of your job description and sometimes you may be paid extra for it (a valuable bonus for hard-up researchers). You'll have had a lot of experience of being taught, but that doesn't automatically mean you're ready to start teaching yourself. Indeed, many researchers find the prospect of doing some teaching very daunting. There's a danger that you may spend a disproportionate part of your time attending to teaching, and that this can interfere with the progress of your research. There is also a danger that, without guidance, you will emulate the worst aspects of those who have taught you, without realising that there might be better ways of doing things.

Many researchers are heading towards lectureships in colleges or universities, and the chance to start developing your teaching skills can be a valuable spin-off of your time doing research. You may find your experiences of teaching an important part of what you have to offer when it comes to finding your first post after finishing your research.

In this chapter we've included suggestions about the main forms of teaching you're likely to encounter, particularly giving lectures (as this is found by many to be the most intimidating part of starting to teach). We've also given suggestions about supervising students' practical work, organising tutorials, and supporting students in general.

You may look at some of our suggestions about teaching and say to yourself 'these certainly weren't practised by the staff who taught me!'. However, the climate regarding the quality of teaching is changing rapidly now, not least because of the advent of teaching quality assessments in universities in the UK and elsewhere. Researchers who are able to demonstrate that they are effective teachers as well as effective researchers may well find themselves at an advantage in the job market.

36

Learning about teaching

Most researchers in colleges and universities find that they have at least some teaching to do as part of their contracts or conditions – or even to make a little extra money. While they may know a lot about teaching from their experiences on the receiving end of it, it can be quite daunting to try to do it for the first time. We hope the following suggestions will help.

1   **Forget about the teaching – think of the learning.** If you concentrate on what your students are learning, and how it feels to them to be learning it, you'll be well on the way towards helping them learn well.

2   **Find out exactly where 'your bit' fits in.** Most researchers find that their teaching is a particular bit of the whole picture. Find out what proportion it constitutes of the whole course or module, and keep your efforts in perspective.

3   **Think ahead to how your students will be assessed.** We don't suggest spoonfeeding your students with the exact solutions to exam questions they will encounter, but we do suggest not taking them off on major diversions. Give them a good preparation for the level of assessment they will meet.

4   **All eyes are on you!** It need not be as bad as this. Use overhead slides to divert the students' gaze from you. Make sure that your overheads are clearly readable from the back of the room or lecture theatre. If using desktop publishing software, use print sizes of 24 point, or minimum 18 point. Don't put too much on any overhead slide – stick to 'bullet points' rather than sentences, and elaborate on these points in your discussion.

5   **Prepare handouts.** Don't forget that most students learn a lot more from textbooks and handouts than they ever do from lectures or tutorials – didn't you? Prepare simple handouts that cover the basics of the material that students should know.

6   **Don't expect to teach perfectly!** How many of *your* teachers were exemplars of the species? Not many! All you need to try to do is be adequate, for starters. If you find you really enjoy teaching, you may start on the slow journey towards 'perfection' – which only happens occasionally anyway!

7   **Find yourself a mentor.** Essentially, this is a trusted colleague, and someone you can really talk to – maybe someone fairly new to teaching themselves. Tell them about your approaches to teaching, and invite them to be there and to give you their reactions and suggestions.

8   **Remember students are just people who are learning.** They are not an alien species – you were a student yourself once. Treat them as human beings and there's every chance they'll respect you for it. (Some lecturers don't treat them so!).

9   **Move away from formality.** For example, if you've got a tutorial group to direct, few students will resent it if you arrange to have some meetings in the coffee bar (or local pub) instead of Room D607!

10   **Get yourself trained!** Take advantage of staff development workshops on offer to lecturers. Remember that later in your career there is the possibility that you'll do a lot more teaching. Pick up relevant skills every chance you get. They will not be wasted.

37

Supervising labs and workshops

Whereas it's rare that a researcher gets plunged into giving a lecture to a group of 300 students, it is very common for researchers to be involved in organising and supervising student practical work. This can be very rewarding – as well as a useful supplement to income! Here's how to make the most of it.

1   **Do the experiments yourself.** It's always possible to make time to actually run through the things that your students will do (you may already have done them when you were a student). It's far easier thereafter to speak authoritatively about how best to tackle the practical work when you remember doing it yourself recently.

2   **Develop the art of anticipating.** Successful supervision depends a lot on being in the right place at the time when students need your help. Build up your knowledge of the stages at which students are likely to encounter problems, and be ready to step in just at the best possible times.

3   **Build up a portfolio of data.** Know exactly what your students should be finding in their measurements. This helps you give credible and useful comments as you watch them trying the experiments or tasks.

4   **Be there for students.** Be at the lab or workshop before any of your group arrives, and stay till they've all finished. That way, they will regard you as an ongoing resource, and not a drop-in star!

5   **Don't tell them – ask them.** When students ask you questions about the work they're doing, don't just feed them the answers (even when you know them!). Ask them 'leading' questions, to help them on their way towards finding out the answers themselves.

6   **When assessing, concentrate on feedback and not just grades.** The more feedback students receive from you about their practical work, the more they will value your efforts and trust you. Tell them what they did well, and what they could have done differently.

7   **Don't be afraid to say 'I don't know'.** When students ask questions that you don't yet know the answers to, tell them 'I'll get back to you later or next week when I've had a chance to explore your question properly'. They will respect you a lot for this.

8   **Show them how to do things when asked.** This of course depends upon your having done the practical work yourself quite recently. It adds a lot to your credibility if you can (for example) give an on-the-spot demonstration how to use an intricate laboratory instrument. Avoid the temptation to say 'watch this: this is how it should be done'. Develop the art of talking *them* through how to attempt something they haven't done before.

9   **Go easy on students' mistakes.** Help them to see that getting something wrong at first is a perfectly normal and acceptable stage in their learning. Remind students that if and when they themselves go on to do research, learning by getting things wrong at first is still firmly on the agenda!

10 **Be ready for emergencies.** Part of the job of supervising a laboratory or workshop group is to know what to do if something serious goes wrong. Check that you have the phone numbers to ring for medical emergencies, fires, gas leaks, or whatever else may be the primary hazard in the situation concerned.

38

Getting started with assessment

The responsibility of assessing students' work can come as a shock. Most people get plunged into assessing at the deep end without any training in how to do the job. We hope the following suggestions will get you off to a good start.

1   **Make sure you know what are the criteria you are using for marking before you start.** These should have been made available by the person who set the assignment. Find out if there's a marking scheme or if the person who set the tasks can give you some useful insights into the expectations. If not, discuss what kind of criteria to use with a more experienced colleague.

2   **If you are marking papers for the first time, sort them first after an initial read into five piles.** It is normally fairly easy to decide if a script is really awful, pretty bad, average, fairly good or brilliant. You can then start differentiating into grades within those piles.

3   **Give yourself time and space for the job.** Marking when you are not used to it takes a lot longer than you think at first. Block in a good chunk of time – don't try to squeeze assessing in between other things. You will need peace and quiet to concentrate. When you are experienced you may be able to assess work in uncongenial circumstances, but until you are experienced, don't try to do it on trains or in rooms where other activity is going on.

4   **Don't despair.** Marking does become easier and quicker as you get used to it (although it may always be a chore). Remember how useful feedback is for students in helping them to improve.

5   **Talk to your colleagues**. Especially on your first few rounds of assessment, you may not be confident that you are marking to the right standard. Check this out by discussing with more experienced assessors, perhaps by showing them sample best, worst and average scripts, together with any you are uncertain about.

6   **When you are just starting out, don't write on scripts in anything other than a pencil**. Write marks and comments as you think of them – you may not be able to remember them later! If you then change your mind, you can erase your earlier marks and comments. In any case, check whether you are allowed to actually write on the scripts themselves. When work is double marked and in certain other circumstances, it is often forbidden to write anything on the scripts. Use 'post-its' to help you keep track.

7   **Remember that the feedback you give to students can be of paramount importance**. Heavy criticism and sarcasm can be patronising, praise and constructive advice can be supportive and motivating. Students learn so much from being told what they are doing wrong (and right) that it is worth investing as much time as you can spare on this. Try to start and finish with something positive. Try out ways of streamlining your feedback while maintaining its value. Use assignment return sheets and statement banks as appropriate to avoid repeatedly writing the same comments again and again on student work.

8   **Don't let poor work get you down.** Remember that you were probably a high-flying student yourself, and may have been blissfully unaware of the other end of the ability scale.

9   **Don't get too anxious about a mark or two.** Assessment is a pretty inexact art so don't dither too much about whether you give a 57 or a 58. Such minor differences are unlikely to make much difference to a student's overall achievement. (Other than at the borderlines). If in doubt, ask a colleague's advice.

10   **Keep careful records.** It is important that you can justify the marks you have given to students (especially when you have not been able to write on the script) and it is essential that you pass on accurate mark sheets to course/unit/field leaders and to exam boards.

39

Preparing yourself for lecturing

You may find yourself facing the prospect of giving lectures sooner than you expected! You may need to do some lecturing to earn some money – or you may be asked to step in when someone is off sick. The following suggestions may make the prospect less daunting.

1   **Find out where your topics fit into the syllabus.** The more you know about what students will have learned already, the easier it is to avoid boring them by repeating things they already know.

2   **Find out more about the students.** Talk to colleagues who are already working with them. Ask them what sort of class it seems to be. Ask about any aspects of teaching which seem to be working particularly well with them.

3   **Get yourself used to the lecture room.** Go in some evening when it's empty, and find out where the lighting controls are, how the overhead projector works, and how it feels to 'talk to the seats' for a while.

4   **Decide not to imitate the lecturers who taught you.** It's worth trying to emulate the good things you remember, but there's no need to do some of the more boring things you'll also remember! Your students will think more of you if you simply be yourself.

5   **Build in plenty of lead-in time.** Preparing and giving lectures at the last minute is not a good idea – even for experienced lecturers! It can easily take ten hours or much more to prepare a new one-hour lecture. It may take even longer if you're planning to prepare handouts and overheads to support your lecture.

6   **Go to some more lectures!** Most of the lectures you will have been to will have been occasions when you were trying to capture the gist of the lecture. It's worth going to a few more just to observe the good (and bad) ways that different lecturers approach the task of talking to a group of students. Make notes of how they do it.

7   **Remember what it was like when you were a student.** You will probably have learnt a great deal about your subject since you were lectured to on it. And even then, you were probably a 'high flier' – that's why you're researching now. Think of the average student, and plan to pitch your lecture to such students.

8   **Do a dry run.** If possible, get some friends in to role-play the audience. Even better, try to get someone to make a video of you doing your dry run. You can learn a great deal about how you're coming across from watching yourself perform. Practise in an empty lecture room during a quiet time.

9   **Think about your pace.** Some of the worst disasters that happen in lectures are associated either with going far too fast, or (more commonly) devastatingly slowly. The most difficult task when starting to teach is estimating how long a lecture will take. Try to build in some flexibility so you can say more or less, depending on how fast you are covering the material.

10 **Think about your delivery.** You don't need RADA training to be a good lecturer, but you do need to think about how you can project your voice. If the room is very large, you may need a microphone (and should ask for one). Otherwise you can help your voice to carry by standing up, breathing slightly more deeply than normal, addressing the student most distant from you and relaxing. Never shout.

40

Preparing your lectures

We're assuming here that you will already have followed through the suggestions we made regarding 'Preparing yourself to lecture'. Our advice here is meant to help you build on your experiences of your first few lectures (by which time you'll be learning fast).

1 **Find out exactly what your topics will be.** Look at the syllabus and see where it fits in. Dig out any lecture notes you already have, and borrow copies of the most central undergraduate texts on the topics. Make brief notes of the most important parts, and remember to keep references to the sections you will ask students to consult.

2 **Plan your lectures in advance.** Think about *how* you will lecture as much as *what* you will lecture on. Students won't find your lectures effective learning experiences if they are badly structured, difficult to follow, even if the content is brilliant.

3 **You may not need to start with the 'first' lecture.** If you're going to do a series of lectures, it may be preferable to start with a topic you feel confident to lecture on, or where you've got interesting visual backup to support your talk. Getting off to a good start with your students helps you (and them) to feel better about the rest of your series.

4 **Prepare some handout material to support your lecture.** Handout materials are particularly useful if you're feeling nervous, as you can refer students to things in the materials when you need all eyes to be off you for a moment or two!

5 **Think about making your handouts 'interactive'.** For example, include in your handouts tasks for students to do (individually or in twos and threes) during the lecture, with space for them to write down their ideas. When students have put some of themselves into a handout, they value it a lot more than a pristine printed piece that someone has simply given them.

6   **Prepare overhead transparencies to support your lecture.** Don't put too much on any transparency – bullet point lists of main headings are usually enough.

7   **Decide what students should *do* with the content of each overhead.** Sometimes you may intend an overhead to provide them with the main headings on which to make their own notes. Alternatively, you may choose to include copies of your overheads in handout material, so students are spared from having to simply copy your words from the screen.

8   **Build up your store of 'interesting things'.** Students often remember the anecdotes better than the main points of a lecture! Try to collect several points which are amusing or memorable, and which will also help to capture students' attention at key points in your lectures.

9   **Plan to build in time for students to make sense of what they've just been thinking about.** It's easy to think that one just has to keep going for the whole hour, but it's more important to think about what your students should be doing for the time.

10 **Don't over-prepare.** Everyone seems to prepare far more for their first few lectures than they can ever get through. Be modest in your expectations of how much you will cover.

41

Giving your first lectures

The art of lecturing is learned by trying to do it! However, some guidelines can help you start to develop this art. For once, we'll try to give you twenty ideas, not just ten!

1   **Don't be late!** Make sure that you're at the right room at the right time. You don't have to actually start at the advertised time if half the students aren't there yet, but it's important to be seen to be there, ready to start.

2   **Chat to the nearest students while people are settling in.** Ask them 'How's the course going for you so far?' for example. Ask them 'What's your favourite topic so far?' or 'What are the trickiest bits so far?'.

3   **When you're ready to start, capture students' attention.** It's often easier to do this by dimming the lights and showing your first over-head, than by trying to quieten down the pre-lecture chatter by talking loudly.

4   **Introduce yourself, when it's your first lecture with a group.** Say a few words about who you are, where you come from, what you're doing now, and what you plan to do.

5   **Tell your students what they should expect to get out of the lecture.** It's useful to do this using an overhead, so they can see what you're going to do rather than just hear it. Let students know what they should expect to be able to do by the end of the lecture. Find out how many students can do these things already – and adjust your approach accordingly!

6 **Help students to place the lecture in context.** Refer back to previous material (ideally with a short summary of the previous lecture at the beginning) and give them forewarning of how this will relate to material they will cover later.

7 **Let the students know how you are planning the lecture.** Tell them what the lecture will cover and give them signposts so they know where you are going. You might start, for example, with an overhead projector transparency showing your main headings at the beginning of the lecture, and put it back on screen at intervals, pointing to the stage reached. You can use it once more at the end as the basis of your summary. Students who can make sense of the structure of a lecture tend to learn more effectively.

8 **Face the class when using the overhead projector.** Practise in a lecture room using transparencies as an agenda, and talking to each point listed on them. With an overhead projector, you can face the class when talking to a transparency, and by placing a pen on the projector you can draw attention to the particular point on which you are elaborating.

9 **Ask the students how you are doing.** From time to time ask 'Can you hear me?', 'Am I going too fast?', 'Is this making sense to you?'. Listen to the answers and try to respond accordingly.

10 **Give your students things to do.** Just about all students get bored listening for a full hour, so break the session up with small tasks such as problems for students to work out themselves, applying the item you have just described, reading tasks, or small discussion tasks with the students nearest to them. These 'interruptions' will help them to concentrate harder on what you are telling them when you resume.

11 **Use handout material to spare students from copying down lots of information.** It's better to spend time discussing and elaborating on information that students can already read for themselves.

12 **Genuinely solicit students' questions.** Don't just ask 'any questions' as you are picking up your papers at the end of a class. Treat students' questions with courtesy even if they seem very basic to you. Repeat the question so all students can hear, and then answer in a way that doesn't make the questioner feel stupid. Students' questions in lectures are often a good gauge of what they are learning, so value them.

13 **Don't waffle when stuck!** Don't try to bluff your way out of it if you don't know the answers to some of the questions. Tell the questioners that you'll find out the answers to their questions before your next lecture with them – they'll respect you more for this than for trying to invent an answer.

14   **Ask questions of your audience.** Ask the question first, then pick on a student either by pointing, or (if you know them) quoting their name. This means that everyone should be thinking of their answer to your question, and not just the person you happen to end up asking.

15   **Watch the body language of your audience.** You'll soon learn to recognise the symptoms of 'eyes glazing over' when students are becoming passive recipients rather than active participants. That may signal the time for one of your prepared anecdotes.

16   **Don't tolerate poor behaviour.** You don't have to put up with students talking, eating or fooling around in your lectures. Ask them firmly but courteously to desist, and as a last resort, ask them to leave. If they do not do so, you should leave yourself for a short period to give them a cooling down period. Make your standards clear, and students will (normally) abide by them, particularly if you avoid sarcasm, vacillation and spitefulness yourself.

17   **Don't feel you've got to keep going for the full hour.** Sometimes you will have said all you need to say, and still have ten or fifteen minutes in hand. Don't feel you have to waffle on. It may come as a surprise to you, but your students may be quite pleased to finish early occasionally!

18   **Have things for students to do at the end.** If you find that you're finished with time to spare, you may like to give students a final task, such as making a 5-minute summary or mind-map of your lecture, and comparing with their neighbours' attempts.

19   **Bring your lecture to a solid ending.** Keep an eye on the time, and when there are only about 5 minutes to go, start summing up and reminding your students what the principal learning points were from your lecture.

20   **Be your own critical friend.** Within an hour or two of each lecture you give, try to find five minutes to jot down your own notes about what went well, and what could have gone better.

42

Dealing with students

1   **Think hard about your role.** Teaching students is a highly professional job which will make all kinds of new demands on you. You will need to clarify for yourself what you are trying to do and why you are doing it.

2   **Check with the lecturers in charge of the course exactly what they want you to do.** This can help you avoid unnecessary overlaps with things done by them or by other researchers.

3   **Get to know your students.** It can make a big difference to the way your students regard you if you're able to address at least some of them by name.

4   **Don't get too close.** Many of the students you teach will be close to you in age. It may be difficult to get the boundaries right, especially if you socialise excessively with the people for whom you have a responsibility to teach. Many universities have codes of conduct on relationships between staff and students. Remember that your role may include assessment. Whether marking students' coursework or practical scripts, you need to ensure that students see this part of your work as involving no favouritism or subjectivity.

5   **Familiarise yourself with equal opportunities issues.** Make sure that you are aware of the problems that can arise in teaching, and ensure that you provide all students with equivalent opportunities for learning.

6   **Take sensible precautions.** No-one wants to be put in a position where they are accused of harassment, so think about the implications of practice. It is not a great idea to organise meetings with students alone in isolated parts of the building at times when few others are about. You would also be wise to consider carefully your body language and proxemics.

7   **Avoid excessive formality.** Some researchers who teach, because they are under-confident, tend to be over-strict or standoffish. Get the feel of the climate in which you are working, and observe the ways in which your colleagues relate to students so you can pitch it right.

8   **Keep your paperwork tidy!** Avoid getting students' work mixed up in your research papers, and vice versa. It's useful to have a separate filing system for everything to do with your work with students.

9   **Save time by making time.** If you need to be available for students to come and consult you, set up some advertised times (post these on your door or notice board) when you'll be pleased to see them – and be there! This can minimise the interruptions to your research work which could arise from students not knowing when best to approach you.

10   **Consider starting up an appointments system.** For example, you can post up a 'booking sheet' where students can sign their names against time-slots where they can come and see you. Ten minute slots are sufficient for many queries, and if students have bigger problems they can book more than one slot, or make arrangements with you for a longer chunk of your time.

43

Helping students with problems

You may well remember what it felt like to be a student with problems – or possibly you sailed through your time as an undergraduate unscathed? Researchers who deal with students are quite likely to be seen as rather more approachable than older lecturers, and you may find yourself trying to help students with their problems. The following suggestions may help you tackle this difficult task.

1   **Remember you're not a trained counsellor** (unless you are one of course!). It sometimes takes a bit of experience before you know instinctively what sorts of problems where you can try to help students, and which problems really do need expert help.

2   **Remember that students with problems feel bad!** Don't be brusque, unsympathetic or too busy to listen. Even if you find you can't help directly, stop what you're doing and give time to such students – they could be more desperate than they appear to be.

3   **Try to find out exactly what the problem is.** Use 'drawing out' questions to help students get to the heart of their problems. Sometimes, they'll subconsciously (or consciously) hide the real problem until they're quite confident they've got a sympathetic listener.

4   **Establish who the problem really belongs to.** It's very common for people (including students) to worry about problems that simply are not theirs. Just helping them to realise that it's not actually their problem can often be enough to make them feel a lot better.

5   **Remind students that having problems is part of being alive!** Don't be too hard about this, but gently help students to be more aware that there's usually nothing seriously wrong with them just because they have a problem.

6   **Suggest that most problems can be regarded as opportunities to learn something useful.** Most problems are only problems until a satisfactory solution or resolution is worked out, and often seem quite insignificant when looking back later.

7   **Think about whether to suggest a 'negative brainstorm'.** In other words, probe some courses of action which would make the problem much worse. These can often be the basis for steps to take in reverse, to solve the problem.

8   **Know someone who 'can'.** You can't solve all problems for all people yourself, but you can build up your knowledge about the experts who can address particular sorts of problem. Find out all you can about the support services within your university, the Student Union, and in the local community. Build up a list of telephone numbers, and where possible names too.

9   **Make notes of who has which problem, and follow-up.** It's very reassuring to students who have previously approached you with a problem if you give them a cheery greeting and ask how things are going now. Usually the problem will be over – but it's embarrassing if you mix people's problems up!

10   **Build up your list of coping strategies to suggest.** Some problems can't be solved overnight, and what people need then is help in keeping going until things work themselves out. You'll probably have your own repertoire of coping strategies to draw on, but even the most resilient of us can always usefully add a few more to our toolkit of strategies.

44

Running tutorials

Helping to run a programme of tutorials is one of the most likely aspects of teaching researchers can expect to be asked to do. Tutorials may be approached differently to those you remember as an undergraduate. The following suggestions may help you approach the task successfully.

1   **Tutorials normally follow-up a lecture programme.** It's a good idea to try to attend the series of lectures yourself, so you know exactly what students have experienced, and what has and has not been covered by the lecturer. It's best to check that the lecturer is willing for you to sit in on the lectures. Alternatively, arrange for a rotation of students to bring you a copy of their notes after the lectures (which also provides students with practice in 'good' notetaking!).

2   **Students' attitudes to tutorials may need changing.** Students often regard tutorials as an optional extra, and their attendance may be erratic. This makes it harder for you to establish some momentum to a series of tutorials you may be running.

3   **Be punctual and well-prepared.** Even if students turn up late, it's important for you to be seen to be taking tutorials seriously. When as may sometimes happen you have to cancel or postpone a tutorial, make every effort to ensure that students know well in advance – and not when they turn up and find a 'Tutorial Cancelled Today' notice pinned to the door.

4   **You may be running tutorials in parallel with some other researchers.** Of these, some may have run the same series last year. It's well worth finding out as much as you can about everyone's approaches.

5   **Be careful not to pitch the level too high.** You don't have to show your tutees how brilliant you are! It may be a long time since you first studied the topics concerned, and you can easily forget how long it took you to get to grips with them. It's best to cover the basics thoroughly and have your group entirely with you, than to leave them miles behind.

6   **Don't put students down.** You won't like all of your students equally, but it's important not to show your preferences and dislikes. Students can be highly sensitive to snubs or sarcasm, especially if they're feeling insecure.

7   **Don't rock the boat!** Sometimes, the lectures you're following up may not have been at all good. Try to help your tutees understand the subject without saying anything about your impression of how badly it was covered.

8   **Don't monopolise your tutorials.** Don't talk too much. Have things for students to do during your tutorials. Pick up all you can about ways of getting everyone in the group involved. Have practice problems or exercises for students to do during tutorials, and further tasks to do between tutorials if they want or need some extra practice.

9   **If you're marking students' work, concentrate on feedback and not just scores or grades.** With large classes, tutorials may be the only time when students can get expert comment on their work. The more your students find they get out of your tutorials, the better their attitude will become, making it more enjoyable for you too.

10 **Keep good records.** Make notes of who was present, what topics were covered, what main questions were asked, and what sorts of difficulties if any students had. Such records will be very helpful if you're involved in running the same set of tutorials next time round.

45

Invigilating exams

After being an exam candidate yourself many times, you may feel that invigilating exams is a very straightforward task. You could be in for some surprises at what a demanding and responsible job it can be. Here are our suggestions.

1 **Find out exactly when and where the exam is, and get there really early.** You may well find that you're needed to put the question papers on the desks ready for the exam, and if there are seventeen different exams in the same exam hall, this can be quite a task.

2 **Familiarise yourself with the rules and regulations.** If as an invigilator you were party to anything that violated these, you could find yourself caught up in an appeal against an exam result.

3 **Wear soft shoes!** You may remember how irritating it can be to candidates to have their invigilators clunking around the floor all the time – or worse still, squeaking around!

4 **Be kind to the candidates.** Remember that many of them may be a lot more stressed at the exams than you ever were yourself. A friendly smile can do a lot to reassure a nervous candidate.

5 **Double-check the timing of each exam.** Sometimes one exam will finish earlier than a parallel one, and there could be all sorts of repercussions if you didn't notice and let the shorter one run on.

6 **Don't distract the candidates.** Some invigilators have been known to make what seemed like very loud noises just turning the pages of a newspaper.

7 **Be alert to any possibilities of cheating.** If cheating happens successfully, it may be blamed on you! Just the fact that invigilators are being watchful and alert can be enough to prevent students who may have cheated from trying it.

8   **Check out what you're required to do should a student have to leave the exam room.** You may be required to walk around with someone who needs a breath of fresh air to calm down, and can make all the difference to such students by just being friendly and chatting about trivialities. You may also have to escort students to the toilet – this can be difficult and embarrassing, as you may have to try to ensure that they don't cheat when there!

9   **Be ready for candidates.** When the exam is well under way, always carry spare paper or graph sheets around the room with you, and watch for students requiring supplies. It's also useful to have a couple of inexpensive spare pens available for students who suddenly find theirs dried up.

10 **Remind candidates about the march of time.** Clear announcements such as 'There are 30 minutes left now' can be useful reminders to candidates who have lost track of the time.

46

Reflecting on teaching

'Recollection in tranquillity' is one of the best ways of learning about your practice. The way we improve our teaching is to constantly review what we do, and develop action points as a result.

1 **Learn from your experience of being taught.** Think back to what made a good or a bad teacher for you, and use this as guidance for your practice in teaching.

2 **Take present opportunities to reflect on how others teach.** Use any chances you can to go to other people's lectures and seminars and observe and make notes about how they do what they do (but tread carefully with any critical feedback you might give – unless asked!).

3 **Invite people to watch you teach.** Let them know what kind of feedback you want and learn from it. If you want them to look at any special aspects of what you do (for example 'How well do I cope with questions?') alert them in advance to such elements, so they can look out for them actively.

4 **Keep careful records of what you do.** Annotate them with comments on what went well and what was less successful. These notes will be really helpful in planning for the next time you teach the topics involved.

5 **Don't be too hard on yourself.** What seems like a disaster to you may not be bad in comparison with others who teach your students.

6 **Learn from student feedback.** Whatever your students tell you will include learning points for you. However, don't allow yourself to get too disheartened by adverse criticism. Students can be very severe on occasion. At the same time, don't just bask in good feedback; learn to build in best-practice elements into your other teaching.

7   **Think about content and process separately.** You might actually teach a wonderful session in which lots of learning takes place, and yet miss substantial parts of the planned subject material. You might need to plan this into subsequent sessions, or look at other ways of covering some of the content (for example by making handout material).

8   **Think about what *didn't* happen, as well as what happened.** Reflect on what else could have been included and what else students might have done during your sessions. In sessions you aren't happy with, congratulate yourself on the disasters that did *not* occur.

9   **Reflect also on other learning situations for students.** For example, keep an eye on the processes whereby students learn in laboratories, practical work, studios, and other contexts.

10   **Remember that when things go badly, it's not always your fault!** Students have lots of other things going on in their lives, and these can affect their behaviour in class. However, take responsibility for those things for which you *are* responsible, and where you have some control.

Chapter 5 Life After Researching

Our final chapter is about things you should be doing towards the end of your time as a research student. The danger is that you may be so busy completing your thesis and getting ready for a viva that you may put off for too long the steps you need to take towards getting yourself a suitable post to follow your research.

It is therefore particularly important that your jobhunting activities are well focused, efficient and productive. Indeed, you'll probably need all the skills and attributes discussed in this chapter again and again in your future career – few people stay for life in the first job they get after gaining a higher degree.

We hope that the suggestions in this book as a whole help you maximise your performance as a researcher, and that this final chapter will help you to sell yourself to those who may wish to employ you.

Happy hunting!

47

Preparing to find your first job

When you are in the final stages of your research, it becomes very easy to put off thinking about what goes after it till the bitter end. A higher degree should not be regarded as a meal ticket! Forethought pays off, and you will find it worthwhile to start thinking about your first job all the way through your last six months or more, even if you don't have a great deal of time to spend on it.

1 **Start early.** You'll be surprised how quickly the time goes. If you're working for a higher degree, the final phases of your time researching will be very busy, so it's useful to get off to a good start with your job-hunting before the busy time is upon you.

2 **Consult careers advisers.** Your university will have a Careers Service of one kind or another for undergraduate students. This service may well extend to postgraduate students. Even if the people running the service don't know your field intimately, they will probably have a good data-base of contact details for major firms and organisations in your area.

3 **Your supervisor may have some good ideas.** Supervisors know what sorts of jobs previous research students have secured, and how they went about seeking them.

4 **Think laterally.** The job you get may not be what you thought you would do when you first set out on your research. There's no harm in changing your plans on the basis of experience and wisdom gained.

5 **Your first job doesn't have to be your ideal job for life!** Don't be too fussy. You may well have a view of what you really want to do in your career, but it may not be possible to jump aboard the bandwagon at any point, and you may need to clock up some other useful experience until the ideal opportunity presents itself.

6   **Consult the trade papers, journals and magazines in your field.** Scan all advertisements till you find out what sorts of papers carry adverts that may be of interest to you later.

7   **Use your network contacts.** Talk to other researchers you know at home and away. Correspond by e-mail with fellow researchers you've got to know through conferences. Sometimes you may end up competing with some of them for the same job, but that's not a good enough reason for shutting yourself off from all your contacts during your jobhunting stage.

8   **Be bold.** When you apply for any job, you've usually got more chance than you might imagine. The only certainty is that if you don't apply for a job, you've got absolutely no chance of getting it!

9   **Be proactive.** Go out and hustle. For example, make appointments to talk to the personnel people in companies and organisations which have the sorts of jobs you may want to apply for. At the very least, you'll be kept informed as and when opportunities arise, and at best, if they really like you, you may find yourself being invited to apply for a job which has really been created just for you!

10   **Build up your jobhunting portfolio.** Collect together your evidence well in advance, including the current version of your CV, lists of publications and references to your work – anything which will give employers a better idea of just what you have to offer them.

48

The application form

People often find filling in application forms a real chore. The temptation is to skimp or rush them, but it's worth investing plenty of time in ensuring that the potential employer gets a really good overview of you. Often the application form alone is used for the initial selection of applicants, with letters and CVs referred to subsequently. Your application form therefore needs to be comprehensive and free-standing, showing you off to best advantage.

1 **Don't put a lot of time into your first approach to an organisation.** Telephone or drop a quick note asking for the form and further details, but don't put a lot of effort in telling the organisation all about yourself in your letter asking for an application form.

2 **When you do happen to have a chance to talk to someone in the first instance, make the most of it.** Often adverts will give a name to contact regarding preliminary enquiries. Ring up the person concerned and ask a few pertinent questions. It gets your name known.

3 **Take two or more photocopies of the application form as soon as you get it.** Use one for practice, and another as an emergency reserve in case you make a serious mistake on the actual copy.

4 **Presentation matters a lot.** Write really neatly if it has to be filled in by hand (black ink is usually required). Avoid crossings-out and don't over-use correction fluid. Writing forms by hand is often a challenging task for those who are much more used to wordprocessing! Good spelling and punctuation count!

5 **Practise with the big boxes before you fill them in.** It is often difficult to fit everything in, so it's a good idea to write out what you want to say first, and then neatly copy it in. This is particularly true of such boxes as 'a brief description of your own abilities and interests'.

6   **Follow *their* instructions!** If they want your data in chronological order, give it to them that way, or however they ask for it. Don't expect people to cross-refer to your CV too readily, occasionally the two main parts of your application may be scrutinised by different people.

7   **Don't omit to fill in any section.** If something is 'not applicable', write this neatly into the box – don't just score the box out. You may find later that there is in fact something you want to put into the box, and it is easier to 'tippex' out two words than cross-hatched lines!

8   **Summarise where appropriate.** It may be the case that under 'work experience' you have lots of part-time and vacation jobs to mention. You don't need to list them all, but can write 'bar work: vacation 1995' or 'retail work, part-time, 1992–6'.

9   **Cherish your referees – you'll probably need them again and again.** Ask their permission before you use them. Keep them informed about the jobs you're applying for – send them a job description to help them be able to explain all the better how you will be able to meet the requirements. Don't forget to thank them, whether you get the job or not.

10   **Think about your envelope!** A large application form, plus a CV and letter of application, can amount to something quite bulky. It will look scruffy if you stuff it multifolded into a small envelope.

49

Your letters of application

While application forms require you to give employers information in the form they required it, and your CV is your opportunity to present information about yourself in the most favourable order, letters of application are your chance to highlight your own special characteristics and personality – it is well worth spending time on these letters! Include a letter of application even if it isn't asked for. Some applications are by letter only (no application forms or CVs), so it is even more important to get the letters right on these occasions.

1   **They've really got to look good.** Use good quality plain A4 paper (never coloured paper, never tiny sheets) and ensure that the layout on the page looks acceptable. Don't crowd the addresses (yours and theirs) at the top of the page. Paragraph the work so that it looks neither cramped nor expansive. (See one of the many books on the subject for good examples.)

2   **To type or to handwrite?** Formerly it was always considered correct to handwrite such letters; in recent years the practice has fallen into disuse, but some employers still expect it. If the advert asks you to apply in your own handwriting, make sure you do this (strangely enough, some employers use graphologists to analyse for personality from handwriting). If you write by hand, put lined paper underneath the plain paper you write on, so you don't wander about the page.

3   **Don't make them too long.** You need a chance to show yourself in a good light, but no potential employer is likely to read more than two or three pages, especially if they have the information elsewhere, in your CV or application forms.

4   **Be guided by the job descriptions if these are available.** If they are looking for particular characteristics or abilities, emphasise your strengths in these areas in such letters. Try to ensure that each paragraph focuses on a particular element from the job description, concentrating on any that are marked as essential rather than desirable.

5   **Get the tone right.** Try to be assertive but not smug. Try to ensure that you let them know how good you are without sounding arrogant. This is often a difficult balance to achieve, so practise and redraft where necessary. Your letter is your chance to explain what *you* can bring to the post and the company. Sell yourself for the job you're seeking, not for a different job.

6   **Be yourself.** Try to let an element of your personality infuse into the letters, rather than simply giving narratives of your abilities and qualities. Your choice of language will be especially important here.

7   **Make sure your letters are 100% accurate.** Employers really do care about spelling, punctuation and grammar. Even if you are good at these it is often useful to get someone else to check letters before you send them.

8   **Show your letters to a friend, partner or supervisor.** Someone else may be able to see where you are underselling yourself or overclaiming, because they have some distance from your task. Listen to their advice.

9   **Start and finish well.** Employers often have to read a large number of applications and the beginnings and endings tend to stick in the mind. It may take you several drafts to get these to say just what you want. Use advice, look at reference texts on jobhunting containing examples of letters of application, to get it right for you.

10 **Keep a copy for yourself.** As with all your job application documents, it is useful to be able to read through again, prior to interview, exactly what you have said about yourself.

50

Your curriculum vitae

An efficiently put-together CV can be invaluable. You can send these out in proactive trawls for employment (even when a job has not been advertised). You can give them or fax them to your contacts to pass on to potential interested parties. It is worthwhile spending time on each successive version of your CV and then making multiple copies to use on all occasions!

1   **Present a good front.** Professional standards are expected with CVs, so if you can't word-process well, get your CV produced by someone who can, even if this means paying for it! As with letters of application, good quality paper is important.

2   **Think about the order.** The components of CVs are all much of a muchness, so tell employers the points you think are most important first.

3   **Tell them how to contact you.** Include in your CV phone contact numbers, home and college addresses, e-mail addresses, and fax numbers as available. It is not unusual for candidates to be called to interview at very short notice, so make it easy for them to find you.

4   **Tell them that you are capable of holding down a job.** As far as you can, without being repetitive, describe in summary form the work experience you have (even vacation and part-time) so that employers know you can get yourself in to work on time and keep on task. You don't have to give too much detail or exact dates, just show potential employers you know how to graft! If you are a mature student, emphasise any particular parts of your work experience that are relevant to the job you're applying for.

5 **Tell them about your research.** The amount of detail you include will depend on the type of job you are applying for. If the jobs are in an area relevant to your research field, then you can give full but succinct details, and perhaps include research papers with your applications. If the jobs are completely unrelated, give the actual title of your research, with a simplified gloss that explains it in laypersons terms. In either case, mention work you have published, and conferences in which you have participated.

6 **Tell them about yourself.** They want to employ rounded well-balanced people, so tell them what you do when you aren't researching. They tend to like especially sports and collaborative activities that demonstrate you are a team person and can be a sociable colleague. Don't overdo, however, the party-animal element!

7 **Tell them about your educational history.** They'll have all the details on the application form (if used) but present the brief version in your CV. If you are a mature student, it's probably worth listing your educational experience in reverse order so the most relevant elements come first. If you came straight from university to research, then chronological order is probably best. Also mention any teaching you've done.

8 **Keep it snappy – aim for one side of A4 paper.** A CV is essentially a 'list of life' so there shouldn't be long, rambling anecdotal elements to it. It is fine to use short and even incomplete sentences where appropriate, so long as it is fully comprehensible.

9 **Keep it up to date.** Nothing looks worse than an out-of-date CV – and they get out of date rapidly. Keep a copy on disc, so that you can alter it as your career and experience develop. You may also want to modify a basic CV for applications to particular employers. Always keep copies of the version of the CV you sent with each application if they vary.

10 **Throw bits away!** As your career progresses, elements of your CV will become superseded by more important skills and experiences. Take out the irrelevant details, and as your CV becomes longer (as you get longer in the tooth), start your CV with a summary.

51

Job interviews

For many people, job interviews can be traumatic occasions, but this need not be the case. Remember that interviews are your chance to find out about employers as well as their chance to look you over. Use them as two-way communication occasions.

1 **Prepare yourself in advance.** Read through everything they send you and use this to prepare you for their questions. The job description is likely to give you lots of clues about what they will want to ask at interview. Go through and try to second-guess what they might ask you – you may be surprised how accurate you are at predicting.

2 **Read through what you have sent.** Try to put yourself in the position of an employer receiving your letter, CV and application form, and look for potential areas on which questions could be based.

3 **Mind the gaps.** The interviewers are particularly likely to look carefully at any long breaks in your CV, and any mismatches between what they have specified in the job description and your own abilities or experience. Try to prepare convincing responses for any questions on these gaps.

4 **Check the look!** Many employers will expect a professional standard of dress, but check out the context and try to conform. In some circumstances it is as much a gaffe to over-dress as it is to look too casual. If in doubt play safe and go for simple, dark, smart, modest clothes.

5 **Stay cool.** It is rare for interviewers to deliberately try to make you flustered, so work with them rather than against them. Mostly they want to help you to relax and be at your ease, so try not to get over-stressed.

6 **Look for the 'secondaries'.** Often, interviewers are working through a list of basic questions which they ask all candidates, but then ask secondary clarifying questions following your responses. These are opportunities for you to show yourself in your best light, so try to answer the secondary questions particularly effectively and convincingly.

7 **Avoid monosyllabic answers to questions.** Interviewers are usually trying to give you opportunities to tell them more about yourself, and one-word answers are rarely helpful unless in response to questions requiring 'yes/no' replies.

8 **Think about your body language.** If you adopt a relaxed, professional pose, you will look calm even if you aren't, so practise sitting in a comfortable stance (not on the edge of your chair or rigid with fear). Try to smile (but not grin maniacally).

9 **Watch their body language too.** You will be able to tell whether you are rambling on too long with your responses if you see boredom in their eyes, or will know whether to continue if they are looking eager. If in doubt, ask 'Would you like me to say more about this, or have you heard enough?'.

10 **Finish well.** When the interview is over, thank your interviewers for their time and try to smile as you leave, giving them a warm feeling about you as you go. (Use this last chance to make a last good impression!)

52

After your interview

Whatever the outcome, you should celebrate having got that far, in your own favourite manner. Later, use the time after the interview to critically reflect on your performance and remember there is no such thing as failure – only feedback.

1 **If you got the job, try to remember and note down what went well.** Note down also anything you were dissatisfied with in your performance, to attend to for future interviews.

2 **If you are offered the chance to get feedback, always accept.** You often learn a lot of useful things about yourself and your performance, which you can put into play at future interviews.

3 **Disengage from further applications.** If you have other applications already in the pipeline, and you have definitely accepted the present job, let the other employers know as soon as possible that you are withdrawing. This may allow other candidates to get a chance for interview. Don't leave it till the last moment to withdraw.

4 **Play straight.** It's bad form to accept a job and then go for other interviews without letting people know what you are doing. It costs a lot of money to interview several candidates, so let a potential employer know if your acceptance of a job is conditional.

5 **Talk to your referees.** Tell them whether you got the job or not, so they know what to keep on your file. They'll be more willing to support applications in the future if you keep them updated.

Particularly if you didn't get the job. . .

6   **Don't be too downhearted.** It's often a very competitive field you are
     working in. Remind yourself that you did well to get as far as an inter-
     view, and that the experience will have been useful to you. There are
     often at least six candidates shortlisted, so your chance on average of
     getting any job is only about one in six. Also remember they don't
     interview no-hopers!

7   **Go through your application and look for any action points you may
     need to take.** You might during the process have become conscious of
     areas you need to improve, or further experience or qualifications you
     may think about gaining.

8   **If you feel you lack experience, get some.** If the reason you didn't get
     the job was because the successful candidate had experience and you
     did not, try to think creatively how you could get into the field. It is
     often possible, through voluntary work, work experience or job shad-
     owing to gain knowledge of the work and context that will be
     relevant in future applications.

9   **Practice makes perfect.** If the problem seems to be your interview
     technique, work on it. Try out practice interviews with anyone who
     will help you (partners, friends, parents, your supervisor). Look for
     hints from them on technique. Ask them to comment on your good
     points as well as your less effective areas, and learn from them.

10   **Try to start straightaway on your next application.** You may well feel
     that there is little incentive at this stage, but the best remedy is to
     work at next steps rather than looking backwards.

Conclusions

The skills needed to be a research student are very different from those needed to be an undergraduate. As a researcher you will have to build up progressively a repertoire of new competences, as well as developing those that helped you get through your first degree.

In ten or twenty years time, you'll look back at your time as a research student with a range of feelings. It will have been a very important stage of your life. It might well have changed your life altogether. There will have been triumphs and disasters – but perhaps there will be disasters which you will have avoided by being alerted to their possibility in advance by this book.

Of course, you cannot expect a book like this to solve all your problems. We do not pretend that if you do everything that we suggest in this book you will sail through your research degree, but we do expect that some things will be made easier by following our tips.

Neither do we purport to tell you how to do research. We think it is simply not possible to do such a thing generically, and that you will need to rely heavily on your supervisor(s), your peers and other appropriate colleagues to give you specific advice on undertaking research within your own particular context. However, the advice in this book has been gleaned from hard experience, not just our own, but that of the colleagues with whom we work, and from the many people who have offered us suggestions, informal and formal, at all stages in our work.

Now you have got as far as the conclusion, it is likely that you have browsed through quite a lot of the book. Some bits will have struck you as common sense, others will have made you think a bit and perhaps one or two items might have provided you with a vital flash of insight. Those people who know our work know that we aim continuously to improve our work, learning particularly from the feedback we get from readers, so why not drop us a line at the University of Northumbria or via our publishers to let us know which were the three most helpful tips here for you, which were the three most irrelevant ones and which three tips that do not yet appear you would suggest for inclusion in a future edition. The sender of the best advice we receive will be offered the prize of a book of their choice from the current Kogan Page catalogue as an incentive. We look forward to hearing from you!

Further reading and useful resources

Useful books by the authors about teaching and learning:

Brown, Sally and Race, Phil (1993) *500 Tips for Tutors*, Kogan Page, London.
Brown, Sally and Knight, Peter (1994) *Assessing Learners in Higher Education*, Kogan Page, London.
Brown, Sally and Race, Phil (1995) *Assess Your Own Teaching Quality*, Kogan Page, London.
Brown, Sally, Earlam, Carolyn and Race, Phil (1995) *500 Tips for Teachers*, Kogan Page, London.
Brown, Sally and Smith, Brenda (eds) (1995) *Research, Teaching and Learning in Higher Education*, Kogan Page, London.
Race, Phil (1992) *500 Tips for Students*, Blackwell, Oxford.
Race, Phil (1992) *53 Interesting Ways to Write Open Learning Materials*, TES, Bristol.
Race, Phil (1993) *Never Mind the Teaching, Feel the Learning*, SEDA Paper 80, Staff and Educational Development Association, Birmingham.
Race, Phil with Ellington, Henry (1993) *Producing Teaching Materials*, Kogan Page, London.
Race, Phil with Percival, Fred and Ellington, Henry (1993) *The Handbook of Educational Technology*, 3rd edn, Kogan Page, London.
Race, Phil, Bourner, Tom and Martin, Viv (1993) *Workshops that Work*, McGraw Hill, London.
Race, Phil (1994) *The Open Learning Handbook*, 2nd edition, Kogan Page, London.
Race, Phil and Smith, Brenda (1995) *500 Tips for Trainers*, Kogan Page, London.

Other selected useful books on teaching:

Brown, George and Atkins, Madeleine (1988) *Effective Teaching in Higher Education*, Routledge, London.
Ramsden, Paul (1992) *Learning to Teach in Higher Education*, Routledge, London.
Gibbs, Graham, Habeshaw, Sue and Habeshaw, Trevor (1992) *53 Interesting Things to do in your Lectures*, TES, Bristol.

Habeshaw, Sue, Habeshaw, Trevor and Gibbs, Graham (1993) *53 Interesting Things to do in your Seminars and Tutorials*, TES, Bristol.

Habeshaw, Sue, Gibbs, Graham and Habeshaw, Trevor (1993) *53 Interesting Ways to Assess Students*, TES, Bristol.

Gibbs, Graham, Habeshaw, Sue and Habeshaw, Trevor (1995) *253 Ideas for Your Teaching*, TES, Bristol.

O'Hagan, Chris (1995) *Empowering Teachers and Learners Through Technology*, SEDA Paper 90, Staff and Educational Development Association, Birmingham.

Rust, Chris (1990) *Teaching in Higher Education: An Induction Pack for New Lecturers*, SEDA Paper 57, Staff and Educational Development Association, Birmingham.

Rust, Chris (1991) *Surviving the First Year*, SEDA Paper 65, Staff and Educational Development Association, Birmingham.

Rust, Chris (1992) *Teaching in Higher Education: A Further Induction Pack for New Lecturers*, SEDA Paper 68, Staff and Educational Development Association, Birmingham.

Rust, Chris and Wallace, Jenny (1994) *Helping Students Learn from Each Other*, SEDA Paper 86, Staff and Educational Development Association, Birmingham.

Useful texts on research:

Bell, Judith (1993) *Doing Your Research Project*, 2nd edition, Open University Press, Buckingham.

Burgess, R (ed) (1993) *Postgraduate Education and Training in the Social Sciences: Processes and Products*, Jessica Kingsley, London.

Halstead, B (1995) The PhD System, *Bulletin of the British Psychological Society*, **40**, 99–100.

Phillips, Estelle and Pugh, D S (1994) *How to get a PhD*, 2nd edition, Open University Press, Buckingham.

Phillips, Estelle (1995) The PhD: Learning to do Research, *Bulletin of British Psychological Society*, **32**, 413–14.

Powles, M (1989) *How's the thesis going? Former Postgraduates' and their supervisors' views on lengthy candidature and dropout*, Centre for Study of Higher Education, University of Melbourne.

Salmon, P (1992) *Achieving a PhD: ten students experience*, Trentham Books, Stoke-on-Trent.

Vartuli, S (1982) *The PhD Experience: A woman's point of view*, New York, Praeger.

Wason, P C (1995) Notes on the Supervision of PhDs, *Bulletin of British Psychological Society*, **27**, 25–9.

Index